FAIRFAX OF VIRGINIA
The Forgotten Story of America's only Peerage
1690 – 1960

Hugh Fairfax

Published by Chiselbury Publishing, a division of Woodstock Leasor Limited, 14 Devonia Road, London N1 8JH, United Kingdom

www.chiselbury.com

The moral right of Hugh Fairfax to be identified as the author of this work is asserted.

This is copyright material and must not be copied, reproduced, transferred, distributed, leased, licensed or publicly performed or used in any way except as specifically permitted by the publishers, as allowed under the terms and conditions under which it was purchased or as strictly permitted by applicable copyright law. Any unauthorized distribution or use of this text may be a direct infringement of the publisher's rights and those responsible may be liable in law accordingly.

Chiselbury Publishing hereby exclude all liability to the extent permitted by law for any errors or omissions in this book and for any loss, damage or expense (whether direct or indirect) suffered by any third party relying on any information contained in this book.

A CIP Record for this book is available from the British Library

ISBN: 978-1-916556-35-5

Copyright © 2024 Hugh Fairfax

Previous published privately by the Fairfax Family, London 2017

To
Alexander, Laura, Marina
and
Victoria

Acknowledgements	1
Foreword	5
Introduction	9
Part 1 The Virginia Barons	**19**
1. A Happy Irony	19
2. A Poisoned Chalice	23
3. As One Door Closes…	28
4. The Apex of Power	38
5. The Younger Generation	44
6. A New Broom	49
7. The Virginian Exiles	56
8. The End of the Northern Neck Proprietary	67
9. Bryan Fairfax, 8th Lord Fairfax: A lifetime of change	74
Part 2: Citizens of the Republic	**93**
10. The Bigger Picture	93
11. Thomas the 9th Lord – Plain Mr Fairfax	96
12. The Journey	100
13. Ferdinando Fairfax 1766 – 1820	107
14. The Children of Thomas and Margaret Fairfax	110
Part 3: The Golden West	**118**
15. Charles Snowden Fairfax – The Californian Baron	118
16. Distant Drums of War	130
17. The Duel at Bird's Nest Glen	135
18. The Shadows Lengthen	137
Part 4. Civil War	**142**
19. The Connection	142
20. Gone with the Wind	148
21. Total War	151
22. The Good Doctor	155
23. Dr John to the Rescue	158

24. The Loyalist	161
25. The Trent Affair	163
26. Decline and Fall?	167
Part 5. Beech	**171**
27. A Chance Encounter in Rock Creek Cemetery	171
28. Northampton	173
29. The Grit in the Oyster	179
30. The Long Road	183
31. New York	187
32. The New Century: A Break with the Past	191
33. Romance in the Air!	196
34. The Big Break	200
35. The Fork in the Road	207
	211
36. The Lost Pleiad of the British Galaxy – Restored!	212
Epilogue	**217**
Index	**229**

Acknowledgements

Many years ago when still a schoolboy I chanced upon an untitled and anonymous manuscript at our family home in Berkshire. Thumbing through the tattered and yellowing pages I found a brief account of our family's lives and times in America. Little of the story meant very much to me then and I might not have given it any more thought until at the very end I was struck by this rather sad statement: "The Fairfax's in America, who survived the wreck of health and fortune in that war of ours, are scattered throughout different States. In a grave-yard, on the hill between Alexandria and the ruins of Vaucluse, are a group of tombstones bearing the family names. There is little else, to-day, to tell the passers-by their story in this county called for them."

Now this didn't make much sense to me and seemed at odds with the little we knew of those distant times so far away, so very different and remote from our life in England. True, there had been some mention of a friendship with George Washington and countless acres in Virginia, but there certainly wasn't any mention of sadness and troubles. Perhaps the author had it wrong and who was he or she to know anyway? I might also have wondered why we were English when all these events took place in America. It was quite a mystery, but it did at least get me thinking there was more to our family's story than we could possibly have guessed. Perhaps this was the moment the seeds of my curiosity in our family's long lost American past were first sown.

Many years later I discovered the author to be a cousin of my grandfather, Constance Burton Harrison, who had written it as an address to the New York Historical Society in June 1888. Constance, as I would learn, was a well-known author in the latter part of the 19th Century and the great chronicler of the Fairfax family in America from the Colonial era until that time. She witnessed first-hand the trauma and loss the family experienced during the Civil War and its subsequent decline. Later she would have seen our grandfather's efforts to rebuild his fortune and then his departure from America to England. Although she might have regretted this decision, I hope she would have applauded his determination. Whatever else, without her long forgotten overview of the Fairfax family's history in Virginia, I might never have had the inspiration to write my own account. So I must begin by acknowledging the great debt I owe her and her work. I trust she would have approved of my efforts.

I must also acknowledge with grateful thanks the unstinting support I have received from my good friend the distinguished historian Professor Andrew Jackson O'Shaughnessy, Vice President of the Thomas Jefferson Foundation at Monticello in Virginia and Professor of History at the University of Virginia. As a rank amateur I have been flattered by his words of encouragement and praise over the years since I first began this project.

My gratitude to the many people in Virginia, Maryland, California and beyond who always offer the warmest welcome to this lost son of the South. In particular, Linda Ross and the late Norman Baker of Winchester, Virginia, who guided my brother Rupert and I around Greenway Court, Lord Fairfax's home in the Shenandoah Valley and as far as Thomas, West Virginia to visit the Fairfax Stone, the source of the Potomac River way up in the Allegheny Mountains and the furthest extent of the Northern Neck Proprietary. Also Maral Kalbian, the architectural historian who has carried out valuable research into the remaining buildings at Greenway Court. In Fairfax, our good friend John Mason, former mayor of the City of Fairfax, is always a welcoming figure on our visits to the 'old country', and his ability to open any door has been of great value in my research. My thanks also to Elizabeth Crowell of Fairfax County and Gutav Person at Fort Belvoir. A great deal of work on the Fairfax family in Virginia was carried out by the late Nan and Ross Netherton and their many publications have proved a great source of information and inspiration to me.

I am grateful to my late cousin Gene Roberts of Upper Marlboro, Maryland for allowing me to use his portrait of Thomas, 6th Lord Fairfax, reproduced here. The late John Mitchell, also of Upper Marlboro was also a fountain of knowledge with regard to our relations in Maryland, notably the Snowden family and his absence is always missed.

Without the dogged detective work of Patricia Arrigoni in seeking out the family in England, I might never have discovered Fairfax, California and the remarkable story of Charles Snowden Fairfax. My thanks to her and the Fairfax Historical Society of California, not least its guiding light the late Bill Sagar, with whom I enjoyed a long running correspondence since our visit there in 2002. Bill's knowledge of Charlie Fairfax's life and times during 'San Francisco's Golden Dawn' was second to none and I will ever be grateful for his guidance.

In England, I must begin with Gerry Webb of the Fairfax Society and author of the excellent 'Fairfax of York'. Not only did he provide a template for the title of this book, but also proved with great aplomb the adage that everyone has at least one book in them. The late John Alves, another stalwart of the Fairfax Society, wrote enthusiastically on the Fairfax family in Virginia and we enjoyed many interesting conversations, not least regarding George William and Sally Cary Fairfax's long exile in Bath.

A chance encounter with my kinsman the late General Giles Mills, an Englishman of American origin like me, provided a great deal of material and insight into our shared history in Prince George's County, Maryland.

Annie Kemkaran-Smith, the curator at Leeds Castle in Kent, has kindly guided me around this former family home on many occasions and provided access to several family portraits reproduced here.

Thanks also to my diligent editor and old friend Henry, Lord Norreys and to my friends and family who have taken the time to read through the various drafts. My goddaughter Imogen Clowes undertook the excellent graphic work, including the cover design, map and family tree.

Finally I would like to thank my family for their wholehearted support and patience over the long years it has taken me to complete this work, not least my brother Rupert, without whose significant material support none of this might have been possible. To him I will be ever grateful for his belief in me.

Everyone finds their own family history fascinating and I am doubly lucky in having a particularly interesting and unusual story to tell, that touches on so many of the big events of American history. I am aware that some aspects of this, such as the Fairfax family's close association with the Washington's are by no means forgotten in America and I apologise if I bore the reader by repeating them here. For the family living in England however, so much had been forgotten, a failing which I hope this book will now rectify. Whatever else, writing this book has been nothing less than the most thrilling voyage of discovery and I hope you will enjoy reading it as much as I have enjoyed writing it.

Hugh Fairfax

London 2017.

Foreword

By Professor Andrew Jackson O'Shaughnessy

Vice President of the Thomas Jefferson Foundation at Monticello in Virginia and Professor of History at the University of Virginia

Fairfax of Virginia is a book that I have long wished to read concerning the only English family who belonged to the House of Lords to have settled permanently in Colonial America. However, such a book was unavailable since this is a story which has not been written in its entirety covering several generations. There was no parallel for other members of the aristocracy to leave Britain for America. Lord Saye and Sele, the Puritan supporter of Parliament, was invited by John Winthrop to live in Massachusetts. He supposedly declined after asking whether he would be received according to his rank to which the reply was essentially that he would be treated according to his moral character and standing in the church.

The story of the Fairfax family had long raised many questions in my mind which are answered in this engaging book which is written by a direct descendant and a delightful personality Hugh Fairfax. Why would the senior member of one of the leading aristocratic families leave the gilded life and status that they might have enjoyed in England? What happened to the family and their lands during the American Revolution? What ultimately became of the family and where are they today? The answers were more unexpected than one might have anticipated making for a much more fascinating story. The family had once owned Leeds Castle which, with its famous moat that gives the impression of an island, is one of the most popularly featured attractions by the English Tourist Board. It was the site of one of the meetings for the Camp David Accords in 1978. Although Thomas, the 6th Lord Fairfax, was predictably a Loyalist he was able to remain in Virginia during the American Revolution, thanks to his friendship with George Washington and on his death the title passed to a cousin, Bryan, also resident in America. The direct descendants remained living there until the early twentieth century when the author's grandfather returned after the title had been dormant for over a hundred years and almost two centuries abroad.

However, the significance of the Fairfax family was not merely due to the fact that they were aristocrats but that they played prominent roles throughout the history of the United States. Most famously, George Washington fell in love with Sally Fairfax while his half-brother Lawrence was married to Anne Fairfax. There is more than a suspicion that she was the love of his life since he continued writing to her up until his death when she was a Loyalist exile living in Bath in England. Fairfax family patronage played a major role in the early life and career of George Washington. He first entered politics and sat in the Virginia House of Burgesses as a representative of the constituency controlled by Lord Fairfax. He always insisted upon using the expression "my lord" to Bryan Fairfax, the then holder of the title in America, despite the ban on the use of aristocratic titles by the American Constitution. The Fairfax family had owned and developed much of the Northern Neck of Virginia which now includes the suburbs to the west of Washington DC and of course Fairfax, Virginia. They owned more than five million acres with a square mileage greater than modern Wales. They played a prominent role in the gold rush and gave their name to the town of Fairfax in California. They fought in the Mexican War and were active on both sides of the US Civil War. They suffered the economic depression of the post war years but revived their fortune through a combination of personal endeavour and a good marriage, while reclaiming the title in England.

Fairfax benefits from the survival of rich sources for all the generations of the family which are well used to great benefit to tell a memorable and unique story. It documents a remarkable Transatlantic saga but it also tells a story which resonates with the self-image of America. Although undoubtedly privileged in their origins, the most remarkable part of the story is how the family managed to reinvent themselves and to bounce back from the economic plight of the South following the Civil War.

Introduction

There is nothing very remarkable about the suburban town of Maidenhead in the county of Berkshire where I was born and raised. Just twenty-five miles to the west of London, it has always been an unpretentious and business-like place, and was once a staging post for carriages on their way from London to Bath. Although the 1960s and '70s saw many of its pleasant old Victorian buildings torn down and replaced with the ubiquitous shopping precincts, glass office blocks, multi-storey car parks and ring roads that litter England in the name of progress, it still retains some charm: On Maidenhead's more picturesque side the River Thames makes its stately way past elegant half-timbered villas, where in the summer months pleasure boats motor up and down under the dappled shade of the trees that line its banks. Not so long ago Maidenhead had a rather rakish reputation as a place where gentlemen would take their ladies for illicit liaisons and there were various hotels for that purpose, notably the infamous Skindles overlooking the river. Heading upstream you will find the river banks dotted with a number of attractive towns and villages, such as Cookham, Marlow and Henley, while downstream the river glides under Brunel's famous railway bridge and soon comes to Bray, popular with celebrities and boasting three Michelin-starred restaurants, then onto Royal Windsor, Eton College and eventually London.

So it was that shortly after their marriage in the early 1950s my parents, not wanting to be in London nor too far from it, alighted upon another delightful village nearby, Holyport and it was here they began to raise my sister, my two brothers and myself. Holyport is the classic English village, its 'green' bordered on either side by comfortably spaced houses of various shapes and sizes as well as several pubs, and it was here that some of the first games of cricket were played. It was also home to the famous Cadogan Riding School run by Horace Smith and his formidable daughter Sybil. Together they had taught the Queen and Princess Margaret to ride and we too were put under their tutelage, with mixed results.

Home for us was Gay's House, a charming, rambling Georgian house, set away from prying eyes down a lane and approached up a long, gravelled drive, surrounded by a beautiful garden with an orchard and paddocks beyond where our ponies and some rather sleepy looking Friesian cattle lived. The house took its name from the Georgian poet and playwright John Gay, the author of The Beggar's Opera who had supposedly paid for it with the proceeds of running a lottery. Although much altered and enlarged in Victorian times, it still had an elegant charm that was not lost on its younger inhabitants. Our world was the nursery, the garden and the fields beyond, safe and familiar, and would remain so for over thirty years until we all grew up and got married.

Although it meant little to us young children, our father, Thomas, always known as Tom, was in fact the 13th Lord Fairfax of Cameron, a title that had been created in the reign of Charles I in 1627 and we were descended from a distinguished family that could trace its ancestry quite clearly back to the 13th century. But to us, he was just 'Daddy': He had served in the Grenadier Guards in the Second World War but had been invalided out with a serious illness, nephritis or 'Bright's disease' as it is more commonly called. Despite this he led an active life in the House of Lords and was a keen yachtsman, but his health never fully recovered and he died tragically young at the age of only forty, mourned by all as a kind and loving father, husband and friend.

Our mother Sonia, who was still only in her thirties, bore this awful tragedy with the courage and stoicism so typical of her wartime generation. A granddaughter of the 2nd

Marquess of Dufferin and Ava, she too had lost her father at an early age, so the sad situation of raising her family alone was not entirely unfamiliar. As a young woman in the late 1950s, blessed with a 'gamine' beauty, she soon found herself in demand as a fashion model and would frequently appear in the pages of Vogue modelling the 'New Look' for various well-known fashion houses in London. She was also a brilliant pianist and, but for the War, might have gone on to a career as a professional musician. We were the lucky beneficiaries of her prodigious talent and our childhood was accompanied by the ever-present sound of Beethoven, Chopin, Debussy and her favourite, Mozart, drifting up the stairs.

Shortly after her marriage to our father, our mother was appointed as one of the youngest magistrates in the country. This unpaid voluntary role required her regular attendance at the local Magistrates Court in Maidenhead, always referred to as 'the Bench', where she sat in judgment on minor civil cases such as speeding infringements and the licensing of pubs. It became something of a family joke that our friends were warned to slow down when passing Maidenhead on the M4 motorway unless they wanted to suffer the wrath of our mother.

Luckily for us our mother had been left well provided for, so we enjoyed a very comfortable childhood supported by a cast of helpers: Reigning over all was the indomitable Mary who single-handedly kept the huge house spick and span; Roly the cook who produced delicious old-fashioned dishes such as steak and kidney pudding and on special occasions 'Jump for Joy', a particularly rich affair of whipped cream and grated chocolate; Mr Leach the gardener, after whom I happily trailed around the garden all day long; the delightful Mrs Archer, a Raj widow who lived in a bungalow in the garden and drove us to our kindergarten school while we noisily drove her to distraction; Bert, the odd-job man who had served first in the Special Air Service Regiment and then the Fire Brigade, kept us enthralled with stories of an action-packed life. Then of course there was Nanny; Nanny was bliss, an elderly Scottish lady who had looked after children of the Empire in Australia and India and did her best to keep us boys under control. If we were particularly rowdy or just grumpy she would trot out such well-turned phrases as 'You're worse than the bears in the bear garden' and 'Don't make faces, you'll stay like that if the wind changes.' We loved her dearly and when she finally died many years later, we all flew up to Scotland for her funeral. It was one of the saddest days of our lives.

In front of the house was a huge lawn overlooked by an equally huge cedar tree, said to be the oldest in the county, which, according to legend, had been saved by feeding it the blood of an ox. Here we played endless games of cricket in the summer, football in the winter and later when we discovered the delights of the opposite sex, we played croquet with bubbly girls who came to stay. Summer holidays were always spent on the Isle of Wight where we messed about in boats and made life-long friends. When the holidays came to an end we were packed off to boarding school with varying degrees of alacrity, but being only five miles from Eton College it was a simple matter to bicycle home for a spell of rest and recreation when the urge took us.

All in all, our childhood was a happy one despite our father's premature death and privileged though we undoubtedly were, it was not untypical of the life most of our friends enjoyed. Certainly there was nothing to suggest we had sprung from a background any dissimilar to those of us born at the end of Britain's Imperial span. Our father and uncles had all fought in the Second World War and we felt as British as boiled beef and carrots and very proud of it we were too. The War was not too distant and of course we had won! This splendid fact loomed large in our lives: avidly we watched war films, read war comics, built models of Spitfires and listened intently to old soldiers recounting their glory days. I vividly remember Douglas Bader, the legless fighter pilot hero, immortalised in the film Reach for the Sky visiting our school to give a lecture and how awed we were to meet him in the flesh. Then in 1966, to cap it all, we won the Football World Cup against none other than our old adversaries the Germans: Our triumph was complete! So being born British was rather marvellous, despite our economic and military decline, and we went about with a certain battered pride. However, the truth is that England was a fairly backward-looking country trading on its past glories.

As for our own family history, we knew all about our most famous ancestor Sir Thomas Fairfax, or 'Black Tom' as he was popularly known, who had commanded the Parliamentary Army during the English Civil War and with Oliver Cromwell had defeated King Charles I at the Battle of Naseby in 1645. We were justly proud of his skill as a general and principled refusal to sign the King's death warrant. After Cromwell's death, he played an important part in helping General Monck bring about the restoration of Charles II, a wise move given his earlier role as the King's chief enemy!

Earlier still the Fairfax family had played a leading role in the affairs of their native Yorkshire, and many distinguished themselves over the centuries: Sir Nicholas Fairfax, a Knight Hospitaller, was renowned in his day for fighting his way through the besieging Turks at Candia. During the Wars of the Roses, Sir Guy Fairfax was Lord Chief Justice of the King's Bench, while Edward Fairfax translated Tasso's 'Jerusalem Delivered' and is considered along with Spenser the founder of the modern school of English poetry. During the Civil War, Black Tom's cousin Sir William Fairfax of Steeton, in his heroic death before Montgomery Castle, was said to have rivalled the fabled knights of King Arthur: single-handed he dashed into the thick of Lord Byron's army and so encouraged his men that they made one more charge and turned defeat into victory. All in all, there have been twenty-three Lords Fairfax of whom six were knighted and three were generals.

But as to our connection with America there was little or no mention. Now this was decidedly odd, since, as we would later discover, our family had actually lived there, first as prominent colonists and then as American citizens for over 150 years. It was as if the family had fallen victim to some kind of collective amnesia, either by accident or design. The explanation may be quite simple: our grandfather had died when our father was only sixteen and our father had died when we were only children, so apart from our uncle whom we rarely saw, there was no one else who knew much about it. But whatever was the case, you might say the thread of our family history hung very thin indeed.

Had we known it, the clues to our American past were in fact right under our noses, for Gay's House contained a very remarkable treasure trove: a huge library. This extraordinary collection of books occupied the entire wall of a large room on the ground floor where we would gather in the winter months. Silently it bore witness to our family activities, an attractive but largely ignored backdrop. There were books of all shapes, sizes and colours. Some were very large with important gold blocked lettering, others bound in cloth or leather and then there were lots of very ancient printed texts bound in simple paper covers. Occasionally we would pull one out to see what was within and were usually surprised by what we found: those written on parchment with large lumps of sealing wax attached were of course the ones we liked the best!

As the years rolled by, we gradually began to realise that this large collection of books was important, although to what extent largely passed us by. As far as we knew it had always been there and as children do, we accepted its presence unquestioningly. It was not until we had grown up that its true significance became apparent. The library was the collection of our grandfather Albert Fairfax and it represented the fruits of his life's work. Albert, who had been born in straightened circumstances shortly after the end of the American Civil War in Maryland, was to devote his life to restoring the family's fortune and position in the world. In an extraordinary sequence of events, Albert would turn his back on America, the homeland of the Fairfax's for so many generations and once again become an Englishman. Here he would reclaim the family's ancient title that had lain in abeyance for so long and begin to restore the family's fortune. Having achieved these objectives by his middle years, he then set about collecting everything he could that related to the Fairfax family. Fortunately for him and for us, the 1920s and '30s were a very good time to be doing this as the period after the First World War saw many great collections broken up in the wake of that cataclysm.

He bought pictures, silver and objects but most of all he bought books; and what a collection he assembled. There were mediaeval land grants and other legal documents from that time, books on the Fairfax's and books by the Fairfax's, letters, bills, and maps. In fact, anything that he could lay his hands on he acquired to add to his fabulous collection of 'Fairfaxiana'. Not least among the shelves of the library were over 5000 'tracts' or pamphlets produced in the English Civil War of the 1640s as propaganda material, a large and important collection only equalled by the Bodleian Library in Oxford. I am sorry to say that it was these small brown books we found so very uninteresting as children!

Occasionally we had visitors, historians and learned professors, who had heard of the library and were delighted and amazed to find such a rich source of original material under one roof. But these visits were rare and by and large the library was ignored and its secrets left undisturbed. Perhaps the most interesting of these secrets were those that revealed the life and times of our American forebears. There were letters from these Americans to one another and even some to and from George Washington himself. Although by no means a comprehensive account, these letters, papers and books could have provided some colourful insights into the lives of our forebears. However, as children all this meant very little to us, and so it remained throughout our childhood.

It was not until after we left school that the forgotten story of our family's American past finally began to emerge. We began to meet distant relations from America and started to travel there ourselves. On my first visit to Washington DC aged twenty I was dumbstruck by a huge road sign saying 'Fairfax'. How my heart swelled with pride! Not long after and back in home in England, one sunny day I opened the front door to a smiling American lady who posed the question, 'Are you the Lord?' After a moment's reflection as to my spiritual qualities I replied that she was in fact looking at the Lord's younger brother. Our delightful visitor was Patricia Arrigoni who lived in Fairfax, California and was undertaking some research on the family after which her town was named. This was a real surprise as although by then we knew about Fairfax, Virginia, a sprawling suburb of Washington, none of us had ever heard of Fairfax, California. It turned out that this town of Fairfax, a few miles north of the Golden Gate Bridge in Marin County, had been named after our grandfather's uncle Charles, a gold prospector turned politician and a true pioneer of the Golden West.

Here was the truth of our family laid bare at last. For most of the 18th and 19th centuries, while Englishmen were building and ruling the British Empire and enjoying the fruits of the *Pax Britannica*, our ancient and noble family were playing a significant role in the American story as citizens of the Republic. Our history was in fact more Custer's Last Stand than the Charge of the Light Brigade; a very strange discovery for their young descendant born and raised in the English Home Counties on a diet of jingoistic British pride.

America at the time seemed very different and rather remote from our somewhat parochial existence. For a start, the American dream that was beamed into our homes from the TV set was full of excitement and life there seemed bigger, better and a lot more fun. Americans could sometimes seem a little overwhelming, particularly to the more reserved older generation of Englishmen and women, but they had launched rockets to the moon, drove vast cars and ate much more interesting food than us, that arrived ready-made and required no knife or fork with which to eat it. Moreover, the girls were always pretty and the sun never ceased to shine. To my generation growing up in quaint, tweedy, drizzly England in the Sixties and Seventies, despite the rather over hyped myth of 'Swinging London', we seemed to be stuck in the past: America looked like the future. But as we would later discover, it really represented our family's past. The slowly dawning realisation that generations of Fairfax's had played a part in its history was strangely appealing. I wanted to know more.

There were so many questions that swam into my head ... Who were these brave and ambitious souls? Why had they gone there in the first place? What did they do there and why on earth did they finally turn their back on the New World and come back to the Old? More to the point why did none of us know next to nothing about it? It was as if the entire episode had been lost to our family's collective memory; strange indeed for a family so proud of its earlier English history.

This book is the result of that personal voyage of discovery. It has taken me several decades to piece the story together, and what a romantic story it has turned out to be. Our family's American forbears were at one point vast landowners with over five million acres of Virginia. They were closely involved with George Washington and his family; indeed, more than one Fairfax lady married into that illustrious family. They played a leading role in early colonial life, and held important positions in the Virginia Assembly. As was normal in those times and in common with all landowners in the colonies, they had owned slaves but were among the earliest to set them free, long before abolition in either England or America. One went west to California in the Gold Rush and although he found no gold they liked him enough to name a town after him.

Then came the Civil War, so often portrayed as a romantic struggle between North and South, but for the Fairfax family there was nothing very romantic about it. Indeed, its outcome marked a low point for the family; but for the valiant efforts of our grandfather, matters might have stayed that way. Born in Prince George's County, Maryland, he would in time bid farewell to his American homeland and settle in England. Here he would rebuild the family's fortune and reclaim the title dormant for so long. As the last link with the past, he almost overlooked one vital task: Where was the heir? When he finally married my Scottish grandmother in 1922 he was fifty-two years old, but fortune smiled upon this union and today his grandchildren and great-grandchildren number eleven male descendants to carry on the name of Fairfax.

Part 1
The Virginia Barons

1. A Happy Irony

If you look at a map of North America you might be surprised to find any number of neighbourhoods, towns, and cities named Fairfax. Some are just pinpricks upon the map such as the towns of Fairfax in Minnesota, Missouri, Ohio, Oklahoma, South Carolina, South Dakota and West Virginia. However, some are much more important and better known such as Fairfax City, Virginia, Fairfax California and Fairfax Boulevard in Los Angeles. Most famous of all is Fairfax County, Virginia and one of the richest in the whole USA. So just what was it with this name, our family's name? Clearly it held a great deal of significance in America and if nothing else, the Fairfax family had certainly made quite an impression in days gone by. So how did this all come about?

Strangely, the story begins with an earlier member of the Fairfax family who had no connection with America whatsoever, but his actions set in train a course of events that would have far-reaching consequences for his descendants.

The English Civil War of the 1640s, fought between the supporters of King Charles I and those of the English Parliament, was a struggle to decide who governed the country, either the King, by 'Divine Right' or Parliament on behalf of the 'People' - or at least those few who had the right to vote.

After an inconclusive start to the war, Parliament set about reorganising its army and chose as its commander a talented young soldier, Sir Thomas Fairfax. The son of Ferdinando 2nd Lord Fairfax, Black Tom descended from a long line of soldiers. He had learnt his 'trade' serving under

Lord Vere of Tilbury, his future father-in-law, fighting on behalf of the Dutch against the Spanish occupiers in the Low Countries. Parliament's decision to appoint him Captain-General of their army turned out to be a good choice and in due course the King's army was defeated. Not everyone sees Black Tom as a hero but he was a man of principle and firmly believed in Parliamentary rule. When shown the Magna Carta at the Tower of London in 1649, he proclaimed that this was what they had been fighting for. Much to his eternal regret, he failed to stop the King's execution and was soon pushed aside by the dictatorial Oliver Cromwell and his Puritans who ruled England for eleven woeful years.

Fortunately the King's nineteen year-old son, later King Charles II, managed to escape to France where he set up a court in exile at Saint-Germain near Paris. Here he was joined by a band of loyal Royalist supporters, among them Thomas, Lord Culpeper. For these brave men who had lost everything, the future certainly looked very bleak with no prospect of an early return to England, perhaps ever. No doubt at their instigation, the King looked around for some way of helping them.

Although he had lost his kingdom to Cromwell, the King in exile still nominally controlled the colonies in America. Of all the colonies, Virginia was the most 'Royalist' in outlook and many dispossessed Cavaliers had already fled there, so this was the obvious place to establish by Royal Decree a 'colony within a colony' of sorts, where his loyal supporters could settle and start a new life far away across the Atlantic, safe from the grasp of Cromwell's vengeful regime. This was no mere empty gesture, as the colony was well established by this time and offered a practical solution to their plight.

The King consulted the map with his trusted advisers and after much head scratching, they settled upon a suitable location. The place they chose came to be known as the

A Happy Irony

Northern Neck, a narrow stretch of land bordered by the Potomac and Rappahannock rivers and not far from modern day Washington DC. So, on 18th September 1649, and with the stroke of a quill pen, King Charles established the Northern Neck Proprietary, thus granting his loyal supporters in perpetuity *'All the lands within the heads of the falls of the Potomac and Rappahannock Rivers'*. Had any of them known it then, these two rivers began much further away than anyone at the time might have guessed and these few words, created with a flourish by the King's quill pen, would lead to all sorts of trouble in the future.

The concept of creating a Proprietary was not unique in the history of America. Both Maryland and Pennsylvania were established in a similar way by Royal Charter, the former under Leonard Calvert, 2nd Lord Baltimore and the latter under William Penn, after whom the state is named. So when Charles II created the Northern Neck Proprietary, it was not an inspired flight of fancy, he was in fact following historical precedent.

We now jump forward to happier times: it is 1660 and with Cromwell dead, England's experiment with republicanism is at an end. With the help of that ubiquitous kingmaker Sir Thomas, now Lord Fairfax, the monarchy is once more restored and King Charles II sits upon the throne. The original beneficiaries of the Northern Neck Proprietary grant are either dead or have sold out to the Culpeper family. By 1681 we find Lord Culpeper's son is Governor of the Virginia Colony and sole Proprietor of the Northern Neck. When he died in 1689, his entire estate passed to his only legitimate child, his daughter Catherine.

This was quite an inheritance for the young Catherine: not only was she now the Proprietor of the Northern Neck, but also the wonderfully romantic moated Leeds Castle in the county of Kent. Then in 1690, in what must count for a supremely ironic turn of events, Catherine married Thomas the 5th Lord Fairfax, a cousin by descent of the famous Sir Thomas, the great Parliamentary General. So with this marriage the Northern Neck Proprietary, designed as a refuge for defeated Royalist Cavaliers, passed into the Fairfax family, the heirs to their nemesis. One can only wonder what King Charles II would have made of all this!

Catherine's inheritance of the Northern Neck's boundless acres might seem magnificent to us, but the fact was that the inheritance had been tainted by controversy and litigation from the very start and would continue to be so; even Catherine's right to inherit was challenged in court by other members of her family. Although he did not get much credit for it from Catherine, it was largely due to the efforts of her husband Lord Fairfax that their right to ownership of the Proprietary was legally established in the English courts, although their son the 6th Lord would face many years fighting to prove his domain's full extent.

One only has to look at a map of the time to see how this dispute arose. No one had yet explored the hinterland of Virginia and maps were fanciful creations, so it is no wonder that King Charles and his advisers assumed the Potomac and Rappahannock rivers rose no further away than in the Blue Ridge Mountains, from where they flowed down to empty at their widest points into the Chesapeake Bay, so creating the 'Neck'. Of course as explorers began to probe the interior it soon became apparent that these rivers rose much further west than had previously been thought, with the headwaters of the Potomac way up in the distant Appalachians. When the matter was finally settled, it was proved that the Northern Neck Proprietary, *'All the lands within the heads of the falls of the Potomac and Rappahannock Rivers'*, as King Charles II had defined it, totalled well over five million acres, an almost unimaginable amount, and it was here that Thomas 6th Lord Fairfax would one day settle as ruler of his vast domain.

2. A Poisoned Chalice

On 9th December 1781, two months after General George Washington's defeat of the British Army under Lord Cornwallis at Yorktown, the eighty-eight year-old Lord Fairfax died in a remote homestead in the Shenandoah Valley of Virginia, surrounded by the bear, the wolf, the eagle and the coyote, not to mention the terrifying shadows of Native Americans. Mourned by many and not least his old friend George Washington, he died far from the place of his birth, Leeds Castle in Kent, and a million miles from the social milieu he had once taken for granted in England.

Thomas had been born on the 22nd October 1693 in the sixth year of the reign of Queen Mary and her Dutch husband William of Orange, the Protestants who had displaced Mary's Catholic father James II in the 'Glorious Revolution' of 1688. His birth came just three years after the Battle of the Boyne, when the exiled James II was defeated by the new King outside Dublin (thus giving the name to the Protestant 'Orangemen'). It also came a year after the Massacre of Glencoe, when members of the Macdonald clan were brutally killed by Government troops in the Highlands of Scotland. The Jacobite cause would be carried on for many years to come, culminating in the adventures of James II's grandson 'Bonnie Prince Charlie' or the 'Young Pretender', until his defeat at Culloden in 1746. However, far away from these distant struggles on Britain's Celtic fringe, there was a growing sense of stability and economic prosperity - at least for some. Life at Leeds Castle must have been very comfortable for the parents of the young Thomas who by all accounts certainly lived in great state there, perhaps too much so, as we shall see.

Leeds Castle has often been called, 'The loveliest castle in the world', picturesquely situated on two islands in the River

Len not far from Maidstone in Kent. It has a fascinating history, originating as a wooden fort built by William the Conqueror. Edward I built the 'Gloriette' (a small fortified tower) on the smallest island in honour of his wife Queen Eleanor. Subsequent medieval Queens to have lived there were Queen Isabella, Anne of Bohemia, Joan of Navarre and Catherine de Valois. Later Henry VIII converted the castle into a royal palace and installed his first wife Catherine of Aragon there. In due course it came into the possession of the Culpeper family and in 1666 was used to hold Dutch prisoners who set fire to a number of the buildings.

So when the seventeen year-old Thomas inherited the title in 1710, you might reasonably assume that this was a time of great expectation for the young man. As well as Leeds Castle, he was in line to inherit all those untold acres in the Colony of Virginia and from his father, Thomas 5th Lord, the old Fairfax family estates in Yorkshire: Denton near Ilkley and Bilbrough in the Vale of York. The young Lord's inheritance might also have included two other estates, Nun Appleton and Bolton Percy, but his father had been forced to sell these to fund the colossal debts he had racked up - 'two and twenty thousand pounds', a vast sum at the time. So rather than enjoying a carefree youth buoyed up by a golden inheritance, these early years were in fact marred by constant money worries, particularly during his time at Oriel College, Oxford between 1710 and 1713 and they would shortly lead to the sale of the remaining estates in Yorkshire.

Although it would be easy to lay the blame for this dire situation at his father's door, the root of the family's financial problems went back much further. The 1st Lord Fairfax had sensibly 'entailed' the four Yorkshire estates for the benefit of his principal descendants. However, in 1666 the famous Parliamentary General, Black Tom, by then the 3rd Lord, wishing to provide for his only surviving child Mary, broke the entail and divided the estates between her and his cousin Henry, later the 4th Lord.

Unfortunately, Mary or 'Little Moll' as she was affectionately known, made a disastrous marriage to the real villain of the piece, the second Duke of Buckingham. Buckingham was an appalling character, leading an extremely extravagant, rackety life and treating the old General's 'Little Moll' disgracefully. Writing in his 'Life of the Duke of Buckingham' in 1758 Brian Fairfax paints this picture of her: 'She was a most virtuous and pious lady in a vicious age and court. If she had any of the vanities, she had certainly none of the vices of it. The duke and she lived lovingly and decently together, she patiently bearing with those faults in him she could not remedy.' In other words, like so many women before and after her who love a rogue, she found him irresistible and was prepared to put up with his philandering and dissolute behaviour because of his famous wit and charm, seen in the delightful epitaph he penned upon Black Tom's death:

> *Both sexes' virtues were in him combined,*
> *He had the fierceness of the manliest mind,*
> *And all the meekness too of womankind.*
> *He never knew what envy was, or hate,*
> *His soul was filled with worth and honesty,*
> *And with another thing quite out of date,*
> *Called Modesty.*

However, it was his extravagance that was to have lasting and disastrous consequences for the Fairfax's.

Despite inheriting a vast fortune himself and marrying the landed Mary, by the time of his death in 1687 Buckingham was ruined both in fortune and reputation. Poor Mary was to outlive him by many years and would bear the consequences of his behaviour. In 1700 she attempted to sell the estates of Nun Appleton and Bolton Percy in which she had a life interest, but was thwarted by her cousin Thomas, 5th Lord, the intended beneficiary after her death. When she died in 1704, Thomas inherited all four estates but the damage had been done and in 1708, the last year of his life, he sold the Nun Appleton and Bolton Percy estates in order to save Denton and Bilbrough.

If the new Lord Fairfax thought this would be the end of the family's troubles he was to be disappointed. Throughout his early years, and as previously noted, especially during his time as an undergraduate at Oxford, creditors continued to press for settlement. This was a constant worry for him and his mother at Leeds Castle and they looked at every option. In 1712 his cousin Brian Fairfax wrote to the young Lord Fairfax: 'Both the wings of Appleton house are down. Writings to it and Bolton, showing your title, are at Denton…a £20,000 fortune would redeem Appleton and Bolton; that, the money for that in Virginia, would raise you to purpose.' In other words, the possibility of selling the Northern Neck was discussed by the trustees, but this was vetoed by his mother. Eventually in 1716 the family was forced to sell the remaining estates in Yorkshire too, finally bringing down the curtain on the Fairfax family's long history in Yorkshire. *Sic transit gloria*.

The purchaser of the Nun Appleton and Bolton Percy estates was Alderman William Milner of Leeds, known as 'Alderman Million', whose descendants lived there until recent times. Denton was purchased by another rich Leeds merchant, Henry Ibbetson, but more happily Bilbrough went to Lord Fairfax's trustee and kinsman Admiral Robert Fairfax, the head of the Steeton branch of the family. Admiral Fairfax was famous in his own right as one of the captains responsible for capturing Gibraltar in 1704 - for which he received a fabulous silver gilt tankard, now at Fairfax House in York. So the Fairfax name did not entirely disappear from Yorkshire and indeed this branch of the family continued to live there right up to modern times.

3. As One Door Closes…

1719 was a significant year for many. It was the year of the South Sea Bubble, an extraordinary period of financial madness that finally collapsed in 1720 leaving many formerly well-heeled individuals penniless. It was also the year Daniel Defoe published his book, 'The Life and Strange Surprising Adventures of Robinson Crusoe of York, Mariner', regarded by many as one of the greatest novels in English literature and still enjoyed today. The themes of monetary loss and foreign adventure were to have echoes in the young Lord Fairfax's life too, but in this year there were other more pressing matters for him to attend to. It was the year his mother died and he finally took on the mantle of head of the family, with all the problems that were to come with it.

The loss of the Yorkshire estates was a great blow to his prestige and he urgently needed to repair the damage done and rebuild his fortune. There were few routes available in early Georgian England to wealth but the two most obvious were through political patronage or by making a good marriage. So the young Lord sought both. This was of course an age of nepotism and political chicanery that would make the most corrupt modern politician blanche. By 1721 and now in the reign of George I, we find the twenty-eight year-old Lord Fairfax following in his father's footsteps as a cornet in the Life Guards, an appointment paid for by his mother shortly before her death. He was also appointed Treasurer to the Royal Household serving under the Lord Chamberlain, a post he no doubt obtained through his family's connections. However, with the accession of Sir Robert Walpole's Government he lost favour and his brief career in politics came to an end.

As One Door Closes...

It was also at this time he fell in love and set his heart on marriage. Unfortunately, and to his immense sorrow, the object of his affection jilted him, preferring, so it was said, 'the higher honour of being a duchess'. This is interesting, as in setting her sights so high, it would seem her attractions were not just physical but also of a financial nature. This rejection is often cited as the main reason he abandoned England for America, but the truth is probably rather more prosaic. What is not in doubt is that he was deeply upset by this rejection and ever afterwards shunned the company of women.

Broken hearted and thwarted in his choice of career, he returned to Leeds Castle where he remained for several years, living the life of an English squire. However, far away across the stormy Atlantic in the colony of Virginia, events began to stir that would have long lasting consequences for Lord Fairfax and indeed many generations of the family to come.

Until then Lord Fairfax had not paid much attention to his immense landholdings in the distant Virginia Colony, although the income of £500 per annum he received from it was clearly welcome, however modest. This might seem surprising to the modern reader as one would imagine that such a vast inheritance might just make the lucky owner sit up and take an interest. But of course, if America seemed remote to a young English schoolboy in the 1960s it must have seemed impossibly so in the 1700s. Just getting there was a dangerous and lengthy undertaking that could take weeks if not months. So when the forty-two year-old Lord Fairfax set off in 1735 to Virginia it was not a spur of the moment decision. As the owner of the beautiful Leeds Castle one imagines he enjoyed a pleasant life there and no doubt here he would have stayed for the remainder of his days had events far away not roused him from his rural idyll. After all, why would anybody in his position want to leave such convivial surroundings and set out for the New World, risking life and limb in the process? Whatever it was that spurred this decision was obviously of grave importance.

Thomas Fairfax's relations with his mother were never easy and much of this seems to stem from the appalling legacy of debt his father left after his death in 1710. Despite his laudable work in preserving the Northern Neck for the family, his widow Catherine (Culpeper) was horrified by his incompetence and never trusted anyone again, not even her own son, Thomas 6th Lord Fairfax. So when she died in 1719, instead of passing the ownership of the Northern Neck directly to him, it was put in the hands of her chosen trustees, Colonel William Cage and Edward Filmer, with Thomas as the lifetime beneficiary. They in turn had devolved the day to day running of the Proprietary to Colonel Robert Carter, their agent in Virginia, who had been in charge on and off since 1702 and this is how it was administered for the next dozen years.

Robert 'King' Carter was an ambitious man who made the most of his position as the Fairfax's agent. Born at Cortoman Plantation in Lancaster County Virginia in 1662, Carter was to become one of the richest men in the colony. At the time of his death in 1732 he had amassed a fortune of 300,000 acres, 1000 slaves and £10,000 in cash. He was agent to the Fairfax's from 1702-1711 and again from 1722-1732, during which time he had acquired large tracts of land including the 6000 acre Nomini Hall plantation from Colonel Nicholas Spencer, a cousin of the Culpepers. As is frequently the case with men who make a great fortune, he became active in politics too, having entered the General Assembly of Virginia as a Burgess from Lancaster County in 1690 and, as President of the Governor's Council, he served as acting Governor of Virginia from 1726 -27.

Carter was not known as 'King' for nothing and whether he always acted in the best interests of his employers is another matter. He parcelled out land to his allies and often kept the best for himself and his family. In many ways he was a prototype 'Robber Baron'. More to the point, his autocratic behaviour had made him many enemies among Virginia's ruling class and his death in 1732 coincided with an open challenge that went right to the heart of the Northern Neck Proprietary's very foundation.

The dawning realisation that the family's hands-off approach to its Virginian estates had been a mistake was by now sinking in; there was clear evidence that Carter had been taking advantage of his position as agent. For a start, the rents of £500 returned to Lord Fairfax seemed suspiciously small for all the activity reported to be taking place in Virginia and when he read Carter's will he was utterly shocked: £10,000 was a vast sum at a time when a well-paid senior Crown appointee might expect £200 a year!

However, what finally brought matters to a head was a much more serious threat: the Assembly of Virginia, infuriated by Carter's high-handed behaviour and rapacious land grabs, issued a petition to the Privy Council in London in 1730 with the aim of restricting the activities, power and boundaries of the Proprietary. This spelt real trouble for Lord Fairfax and when news of this reached him at Leeds Castle he realised that swift and decisive action was called for, if he was to save his Virginian inheritance.

Fairfax's first step was to appoint a reliable and loyal agent who, unlike the late 'King' Carter, could be trusted to safeguard the Proprietor's interests. Blood being thicker than water, he turned to his boyhood friend and first cousin William Fairfax and appointed him agent. William was a remarkably able man: the son of Lord Fairfax's uncle, Henry Fairfax of Toulston in Yorkshire (1659 – 1708), he was born in England in 1691 at Newton Kyme near Tadcaster in Yorkshire. As a young man he had served in the Royal Navy under his kinsman Admiral Robert Fairfax, who captained a ship at the capture of Gibraltar in 1704. By now he had a proven track record as a colonial administrator. He had served as Customs Collector in Barbados and held the same position at Salem and Marblehead in Massachusetts; so it was not hard for Fairfax to have him appointed to that role in the Northern Neck, where he duly assumed the lucrative position of Collector of Customs for South Potomac in 1732.

As I write this, I have before me the original parchment deed of appointment to this important post, which had lain for many long years folded away in a box of papers. How remarkable that it had survived for nearly three centuries and remains in the possession of William Fairfax's direct descendants today.

Signed and sealed in London by 'T Fairfax, H Hale, J Evelyn and John Hill' and dated 24th November 1733, it is countersigned by 'William Gooch Lt Governor at Williamsburg, Virginia on 4th July 1734'. The deed specifies that 'William Fairfax Esq.is deputed and Impowered (sic) to receive all Rates and Duties and Impositions arising and growing due to His Majesty at South Potomac in Virginia in America by virtue of the said act…he has power to enter into any Ship, Bottom, Boat, or other vessel; as also into any Shop, House, Warehouse, Hostelry or other place whatsoever to make Diligent Search into any Trunk, Chest, Pack, Case, Truss or any other Parcel or Package whatsoever for any Goods Wares or Merchandise prohibited to be Imported or Exported or whereof the Customs or other Duties have not been duly paid…'

Fairfax then swiftly countered the Virginia Assembly's writ to the Privy Council with a counter plea that the bounds of the Northern Neck Proprietary grant be established once and for all. This was duly granted and in 1733 the Privy Council instructed the Governor of Virginia to appoint commissioners on behalf of the Crown who were to 'Survey and settle the marks and boundaries' of the Proprietary within two years. Thus began the historic case of Fairfax vs. Virginia although the two years specified were wildly optimistic and the case would actually drag on for another twelve years.

His prompt action certainly stemmed the damage for now, but he realised that if he was to establish his position as the Proprietor beyond all doubt, there was no avoiding his presence in Virginia. So in March 1735 he bade farewell to his family and set sail for his distant possessions across the storm-tossed ocean. As his ship finally sailed up Chesapeake Bay past the thickly wooded shore, Lord Fairfax at last caught sight of his Virginian lands for the very first time.

Although large areas of Virginia were still wilderness, thriving settlements around the Tidewater were by now well established and great fortunes were being made on the back of the booming tobacco business and a plentiful supply of cheap labour. Transported convicts from England, obliged to serve seven years, were a ready source of labour, supplemented by an ever-growing number of black slaves. As well as the Carters, other early settler families were beginning to prosper, among them the Lees and the Washington's, and of course the descendants of both these families would go on to achieve great things in the future. The head of the Washington family was the physically powerful Augustine 'Gus' Washington. Gus was a man with a finger in many pies such as iron ore mining and smelting and he had acquired numerous landholdings including the 2,500 acre 'Little Hunting Creek Tract', later to be forever famous as Mount Vernon. The fortunes of the Fairfax's and the Washington's were to become closely intermingled in the coming years. Lawrence, a son by Gus's first marriage, would marry a Fairfax: Anne, the daughter of Colonel William Fairfax. However it is a son by his second wife Mary Ball whom we remember best. This young man would gain his first employment as a surveyor under Lord Fairfax, but history remembers him for another reason all together. For it would be his destiny to change the world and create a nation that would one day become the mightiest ever seen. And the name of this three year-old? Well, it was George of course!

Fairfax's arrival caused quite a stir in what passed for Virginian society. Not many members of the aristocracy made the long journey to the Colony and despite his low-key demeanour, his presence hardly went unnoticed. However, this was no social call; the Proprietor was there on business and he lost no time in getting down to hard tacks. In October he made his way with his new agent William Fairfax to meet the Governor, Sir William Gooch at Williamsburg, the colonial capital. Gooch was allied with the 'anti Northern Neck Proprietary lobby' in the Assembly who were nervous that the newly arrived Proprietor would upset their cosy clique. Chief among their concerns was the fear that a successful outcome for the Proprietor would have a detrimental effect upon the Colony's income and influence, while at the same time calling into question the legality of earlier land grants. Fairfax was obviously expecting trouble and had not come unprepared. He presented Gooch with the Privy Council's order of 1733, he also carried with him a letter from the Lords Commissioner of Trade and Plantations, signed by the Duke of Newcastle, requesting Gooch 'to do him (Fairfax) what service you can…by preventing as much as may be any unnecessary difficulties or delays in the despatch of his business and by assisting him with your good offices whenever his Lordship shall have occasion for them.' There was no arguing with such a command and the commission to survey the boundaries of the Proprietary was duly created, with agreement that the work would start work as soon as possible.

Gooch tried to persuade Fairfax to accept as final whatever the findings of the survey turned out to be, but suspecting a plot, he insisted that the Privy Council in London must have the final say. He also realised his best hope for a fair outcome was to appoint his own commissioners and chose three men who could be trusted: his cousin and agent William Fairfax, Charles Carter, a son of 'King' Carter and Colonel William Beverley. At the same time and perhaps to placate the Assembly, Fairfax agreed to the legality of earlier land grants and a law was passed to this effect. In return the Assembly formally acknowledged Fairfax as the rightful owner of the Proprietary, although technically he was only the 'life tenant' of the trust his cautious mother had set up, so both parties came away satisfied.

So as the joint commission finally set forth up the two rivers to begin the survey, Fairfax travelled over the Blue Ridge Mountains into the Shenandoah Valley and there, captivated by its wild beauty, decided that one day this was where he would settle. With the help of the surveyor John Warner, Fairfax executed a number of land grants to himself, establishing the Manor of Leeds in what are today Fauquier, Warren and Clarke Counties. Warner would later play a vital part in the boundary dispute, for it was his map that would finally be accepted by the Privy Council as defining the Proprietary's full extent.

Many years were to pass before this dream was to become a reality. With the surveys complete but no agreement reached, Fairfax decided to return to London and deal directly with the Privy Council himself. So in the autumn of 1737 he closed the Proprietor's office and bade a discreet farewell to Virginia. It was to be another ten long years before he returned, but then it would be in triumph, and forever.

Once back in England, Fairfax set about proving his case, but if he had hoped for a swift decision from the Privy Council, he was to be sorely disappointed. There was nothing straightforward about legal disputes in Georgian England, indeed it all came down to influence and without it progress through the labyrinthine corridors of power was painfully slow. Although he gained an audience with the Committee for Trade and Plantations in 1738, his case would drag on for another seven years. The Whigs led by Robert Walpole were no friends of Fairfax and while they remained in power there would be no early resolution to the dispute. But then in 1742 fate suddenly took a hand as so often it does in politics, when the curiously named 'War of Jenkin's Ear' broke out with the Spanish. The ear in question belonged to a naval captain or rather a pirate, one Robert Jenkins, who claimed it was cut off by a Spaniard during a routine inspection of his ship. However, one man's loss was another's gain and when the British fleet suffered a humiliating defeat at the Battle of Cartagena de Indias, off modern-day Guatemala, Walpole's corrupt and incompetent government finally collapsed. The ensuing change of government proved excellent news for Fairfax, and with his old friends the Duke of Newcastle and his brother Henry Pelham now in power, a renewed purpose at last returned to the long drawn-out case of Fairfax vs. Virginia.

In the final analysis. the dispute hinged on which of the two competing surveys showed the full extent of the Proprietary: the Virginia Assembly's or Lord Fairfax's, as shown in the famous map drawn up by John Warner. As Fairfax pointed out, the original grant had come from the King and the King's words could not be disputed. The Proprietary's boundaries were to be, 'Within the heads of the falls of the Potomac and Rappahannock Rivers'.

After a careful examination of the evidence and with the King's word ringing in their ears, on 11th April 1745 the Privy Counsellors at last pronounced their verdict: to Fairfax's undoubted satisfaction, it was stated that the boundary be drawn from the first spring of the Conway, a small stream that feeds into the Rapidan, which in turn becomes the Rappahannock, to the first spring of the Cohongarooton, now known as the northern branch of the

Upper Potomac River, which eventually feeds into the Potomac. All the lands within these borders were now confirmed as the legal extent of the Northern Neck Proprietary - a total of 5,282,000 acres or 8,253 square miles, which to put it into perspective, covers an area somewhat larger than Wales!

At last Fairfax was vindicated and the long years of perseverance had paid off. Now he was determined not to let the Proprietary slip from his control again and resolved to make Virginia his home for the remainder of his life. He was now fifty-five, so it would have to be now or never, particularly bearing in mind that life expectancy in those days for men was a mere thirty-one years, perhaps rather more for the aristocracy. Had he known he would live for another thirty-three years to the grand old age of eighty-eight, he would have been amazed. So, he duly gave his interest in Leeds Castle to his brother Robert, who had recently married an heiress, Martha Collins. As the granddaughter of the banker Sir Francis Child, she provided a colossal dowry of £30,000, quite enough at the time to maintain a castle such as Leeds. Two of his sisters were married, Frances into the Martin family (of whom we shall hear much more later), while another much-loved sister Mary had sadly died in 1739. One by one, the excuses for remaining at Leeds disappeared and in the spring of 1747, doubtless with a heavy heart, he bade a final *adieu* to his family and to Leeds Castle and set sail for a new life in Virginia.

4. The Apex of Power

William Fairfax had not been idle during his cousin's long absence in England. An efficient businessman, he had prospered through his positions as both the agent for the North Neck Proprietary and Collector of Customs for South Potomac. These positions were of vital importance to both Fairfax and the Crown, and in return for his loyal and effective service William soon became a very rich man. As the Chief Military Officer of Fairfax County, which had been created in 1742 in honour of Lord Fairfax, he was entitled to the rank of Colonel and as President of the Governor's Council in Williamsburg he controlled every aspect of the administration in Virginia. He was at the very apex of power in the colony.

From his two marriages, his children built alliances that would increase the family's power and influence in the colony. His first was to Sarah Walker, the daughter of Major Thomas Walker, whom he married in Nassau in the Bahamas in 1723. This proved to be a very fruitful marriage and she bore him five children. The eldest, George William, was always destined to follow in his father's footsteps although, as we shall see, his life turned out rather differently to what had been anticipated. The second son Thomas, a midshipman in the Navy, was killed in action against the French off Madras in 1746 aged 20. The eldest daughter Ann was to marry George Washington's elder half-brother Lawrence and thus became the mistress of Mount Vernon before Martha Washington. After Lawrence's death in 1752, Ann Fairfax then married George Lee of Mount Pleasant, Virginia; a later member of that family being General Robert E. Lee, the celebrated Confederate General. Then there was a William and finally Sarah who married Major John Carlyle of Carlyle House in Alexandria, Virginia. Their granddaughter Margaret Herbert would marry her cousin Thomas the 9th Lord Fairfax and from this marriage our family descends.

After Sarah's death in 1731, William then married Deborah Clarke of Salem, Massachusetts, who bore him three children. The eldest, Bryan, would take Holy Orders and eventually become the 8th Lord Fairfax in 1793. Their second child William Henry was to die valiantly at Quebec fighting under the heroic General Wolfe. Their daughter Hannah would follow a family tradition and also marry a Washington, a cousin of George's, Warner Washington. As we shall see these liaisons with the Washington family would prove their worth in the future.

An outward display of this new-found wealth and position was the wonderful mansion he built on the Potomac and completed in 1741. He named the house Belvoir (pronounced as it is spelt rather than 'Beaver', like the English Castle of that name) and it occupied a magnificent position overlooking the river between Pohick Creek and Dogue Run. This house was an embodiment of his new-found power and wealth.

Although no contemporary images of this splendid house survive, we know it was two storeys high over a full basement and measured 60 by 36 feet. Contemporary accounts tell us that it was furnished to the highest standards of the time, with furniture from London and porcelain from China. This was after all the golden age of British furniture making and it is likely he acquired pieces by Chippendale or Sheraton, so one can only imagine how elegant and sumptuous it must have been. Here he would entertain his friends, neighbours and important guests from England whose ships anchored in the creek below; and when not attending to his duties, he lived the congenial life of an English hunting squire.

But Belvoir was more than just a fine residence, it also served as the nerve centre for the Northern Neck Proprietary, with a purpose-built estate office close to the mansion. There were also other buildings a comfortable distance away that would have housed the slaves. This was a society and economy based on slavery, however distasteful to our sensibilities, but accepted without question in those times.

However, Belvoir's time was fated to be short-lived and well before the end of the century it had returned to dust, a victim of the events that would engulf the colony. An artist's impression of this wonderful house and its elegant gardens shows just what has been lost and if it were still here today would undoubtedly rival other colonial houses of the period. A visit to such neighbouring properties as Gunston Hall or Mount Vernon gives one a very good idea of just how elegant life was for the privileged few in those days. I was lucky enough to be able to visit Fort Belvoir in 2012 – as a military establishment it is hard to get permission to visit these days – and I saw the ruins of the house in a quiet corner of the base. Much excavation has been carried out in the last 100 years and the outline of the house is clearly marked. Not far away there is a memorial obelisk to Colonel William Fairfax, his wife Deborah and two of his sons, William Henry who fell at Quebec and Thomas, who suffered the same fate at Madras.

It was at this point that the young George Washington comes into the Fairfax's' lives for the first time. As agent for the newly arrived Lord Fairfax, Colonel William's main task was to organise the surveying of the Northern Neck for sales of leaseholds to eager settlers. He appointed his own son George William as the principal surveyor and casting around for a reliable assistant, his eye lit on the 16 year-old George Washington. George was no stranger to the Fairfax family, indeed he was related by marriage through his elder half-brother Lawrence who was married to Colonel Fairfax's daughter Ann, and living across the creek at Mount Vernon.

Lord Fairfax himself clearly took a shine to the young man, writing to his mother Mary Washington: *'Young George has what my friend, Mr Addison, was pleased to call the intellectual conscience. The Lord deliver him from the nets of those spiders, called women, who will cast for his ruin. I wish I could say that he governs his temper for he is subject to attacks of anger on provocation, and sometime without just cause, But time will cure him.'* It seems poor Lord Fairfax had never got over being jilted as a young man!

The bright and energetic young George seemed a natural choice and so he proved to be, as the young man quickly showed himself a resilient and capable employee, demonstrating all those qualities and talents that would one day place him among the greatest leaders the world has ever seen.

In March 1748, George William Fairfax and George Washington saddled up their horses and set off on their mission to survey Lord Fairfax's lands across the Blue Ridge Mountains in the Shenandoah Valley and the wilds beyond. What a baptism of fire this would be and fortunately the young Washington recorded their adventures in a diary entitled *A Journal of My Journey over the Mountains*. From this we learn much of their incredible adventures: fording swollen rivers, fending off hungry bears, shooting wild turkey and sleeping rough under the stars. Along the way, they met Native Americans, fresh from battle with scalps to prove it. They shared their meals, watched them dance and got drunk! Nothing seems to have fazed Washington, but the same could not be said for George William, whose enthusiasm for the pioneering life of a frontiersman was limited, to say the least, something that did not endear him to his employer and cousin Lord Fairfax.

Belvoir proved to be a very comfortable billet for the newly arrived Lord Fairfax and here he would stay for a couple of years, settling into his new life as the Virginian Proprietor. Aside from his duties, he spent many happy days hunting with his relations and neighbours over the tidewater which teemed with game of all sorts. But Belvoir's location on the Potomac, delightful though it may have been, was increasingly inconvenient for the work of settling the Proprietary; so in 1752 he moved his headquarters deep into the heart of the Shenandoah Valley, far from the comforts of Belvoir. Here on the land he had granted to himself by deed in 1736, the Manor of Leeds, he built his new home below the slopes of the Blue Ridge Mountains, not far from the new town of Winchester. He named it Greenway Court after a family property near Leeds Castle in Kent and although the main house is long gone, several of the outbuildings remain today, including a stone built building, thought to be the estate office where the young George Washington had worked. However recent dendrological research – the study of the building's timbers - carried out by the architectural historian Maral Kalbian has dated this building to 1761, a little after Washington's time there.

On the main road from Ashby's Gap to Winchester, he and his young assistant George Washington erected a large white post from which the modern town of White Post takes its name. A successor to the original still stands today.

It was here at Greenway Court that the relationship between Lord Fairfax and George Washington blossomed, much as that between a tutor and his pupil. On a practical level, the surveying expeditions Washington undertook for his employer taught him much about field craft, skills he would put to good use in his life as a soldier. Perhaps more importantly he also learnt a great deal from the worldly Fairfax, who was only too happy to pass on to his young companion the knowledge and wisdom he had gained over the course of his sixty years. He taught him all he knew about politics, culture and society in Georgian England and George made good use of the extensive library that Fairfax had shipped over from England, absorbing the lessons of history.

It would be very surprising too if the subject of the English Civil War had not arisen during those long months at Greenway Court. It was a pivotal moment in English history and of course Fairfax's famous forebear Sir Thomas, 'Black Tom', had played a key role as Commander in Chief of the victorious Parliamentary army. One wonders if this did not sow a small seed in the impressionable young Washington's mind that one day would grow into thoughts of rebellion against the British Crown? After all, had not the cry '*No Taxation without Representation*' been one of the chief complaints of the English Parliamentarians when they rose in rebellion against King Charles I in 1642? This is of course just conjecture, but what a coincidence that the man who would one day lead the American rebellion should have been schooled by none other than a descendant of one of the leaders of that earlier English rebellion!

Whatever else, this crucial period at Lord Fairfax's side would prove to be the perfect education for the young George Washington and would stand him in good stead for the rigours and challenges of that extraordinary life which lay ahead. It should never be underestimated, although history frequently does, just what a huge influence Lord Fairfax had on his young protégée: one might even go as far as to say that without it, history might have taken a very different course.

5. The Younger Generation

Until now our story has mainly concerned Thomas the 6th Lord Fairfax and his cousin William, but now it is time to meet the younger generation who will carry the story forwards. George William, who we have already briefly met, was the senior member of the family in the next generation and so was in line to inherit the title from his bachelor cousin. He was educated in England where he picked up the airs and graces of an English nobleman and lived in great style at Belvoir. Although he is said to have referred to it rather condescendingly as a *'nice little cottage in this wooded land'*, it was certainly more to his taste than the life of a pioneering frontiersman. He was in many ways the epitome of that fortunate fellow, the son of an ambitious and successful man, and in 1748 he married the beautiful eighteen year-old Sally Cary, daughter of Colonel Wilson Cary of Ceely's Plantation on the James River with one of the greatest fortunes of the colony. Together they made a very elegant couple holding court at Belvoir, although their life together was to turn out in a very different way than they might have imagined at the time.

Perhaps the most intriguing aspect of Sally's life was the close relationship that developed between her and the young George Washington during the 1750's. Living but *'a whoop and a holla'* away from Belvoir at Mount Vernon, George's life had become inextricably linked to the Fairfax's. Not only was he employed as a surveyor, but when time allowed he was a frequent visitor to Belvoir where both families would regularly hunt together. This handsome, brave young pioneer and soldier clearly impressed Sally and he was equally attracted to this attractive, popular and accomplished young woman, who could speak French, was a gifted amateur actress and a knowledgeable gardener. In many ways, she must have seemed to the impressionable young man the paradigm of womanhood, combining both beauty and brains. Historians have long since wondered how far this relationship went and with good reason too, since several of the letters they frequently wrote to one another have survived to tell a tale of barely disguised passion. But given the lofty ideals and morals by which Washington lived, it is unlikely that the relationship was anything other than platonic. Any hint of impropriety would have been devastating to their social standing and quite unpardonable. In any case Sally was married to George William Fairfax and Washington would shortly embark on a happy marriage to the rich widow Martha Dandridge Custis. However, this did not stop Washington penning this remarkable letter to Sally just before he got married.

Writing from '*Camp at Fort Cumberland*' on 12th September 1758 he begins:

'Dear Madam,

> *Yesterday I was honoured with your short, but very agreeable favour of the first instt. How joyfully I catch at the happy occasion of renewing a correspondence, which I feared was dis-relished on your part, I leave to time, that never failing expositor of all things – and to a monitor equally as faithful in my own breast – to testify. In silence I now express my joy...*

> *'tis true, I profess myself a Votary to Love. I acknowledge that a Lady is in the case: and, further, I confess that this Lady is known to you. Yes, Madam, as well as she is to one who is too sensible of her Charms to deny the Power whose influence he feels and must ever submit to. I feel the force of her amiable beauties in the recollection of a thousand tender passages that I wish to obliterate, till I am bid to revive them – but experience alas! sadly reminds me how impossible this is, and evinces an opinion, which I have long entertained, that there is a Destiny which has the sovereign control of our actions, not to be resisted by the strongest efforts of Human Nature.'*

In case Sally fails to decipher his coded feelings, he goes on, drawing her closer to his secret longings:

> *'You have drawn me, my dear Madam, or rather I have drawn myself, in an honest confession of a simple fact. Misconstrue not my meaning, 'tis obvious; doubt it not, nor expose it. The world has no business to know the object of my love, declared in this manner to…you, when I want to conceal it.*
>
> *One thing above all things in this world I wish to know, and only one person of your acquaintance can solve me that or guess my meaning…but adieu to this, 'til happier times if I ever shall see them.'*

In her reply, Sally sensibly fails to respond to his suggestions, so he writes again, this time more plaintively:

> *'Do we misunderstand the true meaning of each other's letters? I think it must appear so, though I would fain hope the contrary, as I cannot speak plainer without…But I'll say no more and leave you to guess the rest.'*

He then goes on to make reference to the play 'Cato' by Joseph Addison in which Juba, a prince of Namibia, falls in love with Cato's daughter Marcia, commenting:

> *'I should think our time more agreeably spent, believe me, in playing a part in Cato with myself doubly happy in being the Juba to a Marcia as must make.'*

Clearly these are the thinly-veiled words of a young man in love, unrequited as it turned out. How sad that this love was never able to manifest itself, but here we will have to leave this poignant tale for now. There is little doubt that Washington would always 'hold a candle' for Sally throughout his life and despite separation, marriages and all the momentous events that would ensue, George and Sally continued to write to each another throughout their lives, as we shall see.

The Younger Generation

More weighty matters were calling upon Washington's attention, and his life is of course well documented so this is not the place to go over them. Suffice to say his early friendship with the Fairfax's was to endure throughout his life, in spite of their finding themselves in opposing camps and on different sides of the Atlantic during the coming Revolution.

Another of Colonel William Fairfax's children to make an important marriage was his daughter Sarah who married John Carlyle in 1747. Their daughter, also Sarah, would marry William Herbert, whose daughter Margaret would in turn marry Thomas Fairfax, her first cousin once removed. Thomas was the son of Bryan 8th Lord Fairfax, and would in turn become the 9th Lord Fairfax. Thus all later generations of the family descend from John and Sarah Carlyle.

John Carlyle (1720–1780) was a Scottish merchant who became a leading landowner and social and political figure in Northern Virginia. He was also a founding trustee and the first overseer of Alexandria, Virginia.

Born in Dumfriesshire in Scotland he had emigrated to Virginia in 1741 as the agent of an English merchant William Hicks. Here he quickly established himself as a merchant at Belhaven, later known as Alexandria, a settlement that had grown up around a tobacco warehouse on the bluffs overlooking the Potomac River.

Carlyle was a real tycoon. His business ventures included trading with England and the West Indies, retail operations in Alexandria, a foundry in the Shenandoah Valley, milling, and the operation of a forge. He also owned thousands of acres of land throughout Virginia, including three plantations.

It did him no harm when he married into the powerful Fairfax family, and he set about building his wife Sarah a house in Alexandria that would reflect this new-found power and status. Carlyle House was completed in 1753 and is unique in being the only stone-built house in Alexandria, a true sign of the its owner's immense wealth.

With the French and Indian War raging on the colony's border in the Ohio Valley, Carlyle was appointed in 1754 a major in the Virginia Militia. When, early the next year, Major-General Edward Braddock was sent to Virginia to lead the campaign against the French and Indian forces, he set up his headquarters at Carlyle House. Braddock convened the 'Congress of Alexandria' at the house, most likely in the dining room, and it was here that the fateful decision to launch an expedition to Fort Duquesne was taken, one which would result in his violent death at the hands of native Americans. Also present at the meeting was the young George Washington who had very nearly met his own end fighting the French and Indians on the Forks of the Ohio River. Washington strongly advised Braddock against the expedition but the British General knew better and blithely ignored the young colonist's advice. That sealed his fate.

John and Sarah's life at Carlyle House was not to last long for she died in January 1761, less than ten years after it was built. Carlyle subsequently married Sybil West, daughter of prominent Alexandrian Hugh West and when he died in 1780, he was buried at the Old Presbyterian Meeting House.

For many years Carlyle House was neglected and forgotten, hidden away behind a hotel, but it has now been beautifully restored to its former glory and is open to the public. Since 1970, the Carlyle House Historic Park has been owned and administered by the Northern Virginia Regional Park Authority and it includes the 18th century Palladian mansion and gardens. Every year the 'Grandest Congress' is re-enacted, celebrating General Braddock's time at Carlyle House.

6. A New Broom

When Lord Fairfax moved his headquarters to Greenway Court in 1752, his long-time agent and cousin Colonel William Fairfax took this as his cue to retire. His son George William had always assumed he would take on this important post, but he was to be disappointed. His lack of enthusiasm for the rough life on the frontier had failed to impress Lord Fairfax who passed him over in favour of his nephew, Thomas Bryan Martin, whom he summoned from England. Thomas was the son of his sister Frances and her husband Denny Martin (the elder), who lived near Leeds Castle. He would prove to be a good choice.

Lord Fairfax was obviously very fond of Frances and her family would in due course become his heirs. Like her brother, she was also to live into her late eighties. She had eight children and several of them were immensely long lived, although remarkably not one ever married.

The eldest was Edward (1723-75), a soldier and landowner in Kent. Then there was John (1724-46), a sailor. Next was Denny (1725 -1800), who would become a clergyman and eventually, Lord Fairfax's heir; there were two very long-lived sisters, Frances (1727-1813), and Sibylla (1729-1816); after them came Thomas Bryan (1731- 98), the agent for Lord Fairfax in succession to Colonel William Fairfax and his long-term companion at Greenway Court. Finally, there was Philip (1733-1821), a Major-General in the British Army, and another sister, Anna Susanna (1736-1817).

The appointment of Thomas Bryan Martin as Lord Fairfax's agent did nothing to improve relations between Lord Fairfax and George William. The pragmatic Lord Fairfax, faced with the huge task of administering his vast empire, picked the most able and trustworthy man he could find. As his nephew, he was of course a closer relation to

Lord Fairfax than George William and despite not being a Fairfax by name, his preferment could hardly be seen as controversial. George William, the native-born Virginian, clearly saw things very differently and over the course of the next two decades this estrangement grew ever more bitter. In the end George William and his wife Sally would leave Virginia for good, living out their final days in England.

Today you can drive from Washington DC to Greenway Court near the peaceful town of Winchester in little more than an hour, but when Lord Fairfax settled there it was truly remote, a long hard ride from the comparative civilisation of the Tidewater settlements. These were dangerous times and quite apart from the ever-present threat of attack from local Native Americans, storm clouds were gathering to the west. Beyond the Appalachians the Natives still roamed free, but their liberty was increasingly under threat. The French had linked their colonies in Canada and Louisiana with a chain of forts and this would soon lead to conflict with the English colonists pushing westward, most noticeably into what is now Ohio. Both sides laid claim to all the territory east of the Mississippi and their ambitions were gathering pace. The Ohio Company had been established for this very purpose in 1747 and was supported by many leading Virginians, such as Thomas Lee, Nathaniel Chapman, John Mercer, George Washington's brothers Lawrence and Augustine, as well as Englishmen such as the Duke of Bedford, Governor of Virginia Robert Dinwiddie and John Hanbury, a wealthy London merchant. As a direct challenge to the French, the Ohio Company built a series of forts on the frontier and before long a number of short and bloody skirmishes ensued, in which Washington, by now a member of the Virginia Militia, played a leading role and very nearly lost his life. He had another lucky escape when in June 1755 General Braddock and his troops were massacred by a combined army of French and Native American allies on the Monongahela River near present day Pittsburgh.

Interestingly, when the great tycoon Andrew Carnegie was building his steel works on this site in the late 1800s, workmen came across the bones of numerous soldiers, doubtless the luckless General's among them...

These early skirmishes soon developed into all-out war, known in America as the 'French and Indian War', an important dimension of the Seven Years' War, when Britain and France fought for dominance across the globe. The conflict raged from America, Canada and Cuba to Europe, India, and even the Philippines.

This was the era of Clive of India and Wolfe of Quebec; General James Wolfe was a real soldier's soldier. Brave yet compassionate, he led from the front. His capture of Quebec at the Battle of the Plains of Abraham on 13th September 1759 was achieved through one of the greatest acts of military derring-do: landing his force of 9000 soldiers and 18,000 sailors from 200 ships at the base of the cliffs west of Quebec on the St Lawrence River, they scaled the cliffs with two small canons and took the Marquis de Montcalm's French army completely by surprise. The battle was over in 15 minutes, but in that time both Wolfe and Montcalm were mortally wounded.

Another young man who fell that day was young William Henry Fairfax, son of Colonel William Fairfax and his wife Deborah. He had served briefly under George Washington in the Virginia Militia and then with his support succeeded in purchasing a commission in Braggs Regiment, the 28th Foot. Legend has it that before the Battle of Quebec, General Wolfe, aware of the young man's famous ancestor Sir Thomas Fairfax, addressed him with these stirring words: *'Young man, when we come into action, remember your name.'* Doubtless he did, but he died on 23rd October from his wounds. It must have been a sad loss to the family but by all accounts he was a gallant soldier whose name we here remember with pride.

The crushing defeat of the French at Quebec, together with their expulsion from Ohio and the capture of Guadeloupe effectively brought the war in North America to a close and secured Canada for the British for ever more. Taken with Clive's success at Madras in India and the defeat of the French at Minden in Germany by a combined Anglo-German force under the command of Prince Ferdinand of Brunswick, 1759 was declared the '*Annus Mirabilis*'. This was the year when Britain finally eclipsed France as a global power and laid the foundation of over two centuries of Anglo-Saxon hegemony.

During these years, life for settlers in the Shenandoah Valley grew ever more precarious and many families were brutally murdered by the Natives, egged on by their French allies. Scalping was widespread and the Redcoats responded with equal ferocity. For a time, the very existence of the Northern Neck Proprietary looked to be in the balance as settlers fled back to the safety of the Tidewater settlements. Lord Fairfax bravely did his best to mollify the tribes, including the ceremonial smoking of peace pipes and exchanging wampum, but in reality there was little he could do. Even Greenway Court came under attack and the stone-built safe house still stands as a reminder of those fearful times.

This carried on throughout the 1750s but with the defeat of the French in 1759 and the Treaty of Paris in 1763, the native tribes lost a strong ally and with it any chance of turning the tide of westward expansion into their lands.

The long-term consequences of the war were another matter altogether and their outcome would be far more dramatic than anyone might have guessed at the time. For the British, the outcome appeared to be very favourable. Canada was now British and the French had been expelled from Nova Scotia or 'Acadia' as it was known to the French. (Many of the French-speaking settlers from this region decamped to Louisiana and gave us the word 'Cajun', short for Acadia.) The French were given Guadeloupe and Martinique in exchange for their northern dominions and the Spanish received Cuba in exchange for Florida. Everybody was happy and settled, victors and vanquished alike, or so it seemed. However, this was to come at a very heavy price to Britain as we shall see in a later chapter.

The cost of the war was enormous and it left Britain with a national debt doubled in size. The remedy seemed obvious from the perspective of London: the colonists should contribute of course, after all it was their land for which the battles were fought and so much blood shed. This meant higher taxes. At the same time, the Royal Proclamation of 1763 which set out provisions for the future administration of the colonies caused further upset with the reservation of the lands to the west of the Appalachian Mountains for native tribes – a decision inexplicable to the colonists who were under the impression that the subjugation of these native lands was the chief reason for the war in the first place! As a result of these measures the embers of resentment glowed red in the hearts and minds of the colonists: in time they would burst into flames.

Throughout this tumult and the continual threat of a sudden and brutal death at the hands of the natives, Lord Fairfax and Thomas Martin steadily continued their work at Greenway Court, issuing land grants and collecting the rents. Slowly but surely, the coffers of the Northern Neck Proprietary were swelling. This was something that had not gone unnoticed by other members of the family, most noticeably the Colonel's son George William. Despite the glittering prospects his early life had promised, his plans were now beginning to go awry.

He had been passed over by Lord Fairfax in favour of his cousin Thomas Martin as agent for the Northern Neck and when his father died in 1757, George William also failed to succeed him in the highly lucrative post of Collector of Customs for South Potomac, which Colonel William had held since 1732. This left him in a very difficult position. Living at Belvoir required large resources and for these he mainly looked to Lord Fairfax at Greenway Court. He did, however, have another source of finance available. When his eccentric, bagpipe-playing uncle Henry died in 1759, George William found himself heir to his uncle's estates of Toulston and Redness in Yorkshire. However, the inheritance was disputed and this would lead to years of litigation. So it was to England he went, and in the 1760s he spent two periods there, intent on securing his inheritance.

The dispute over his inheritance dragged on and when he returned to Virginia in 1768 matters still far from resolved. This time, he was accompanied by Lord Fairfax's younger brother Robert. Both saw themselves as successors to the peerage and Robert would in due course become the 7th Lord Fairfax. However, what really attracted their attention was the growing wealth of the Proprietary, which by 1768 enjoyed an income of £4,000 per annum - a very considerable sum at the time. Robert, like his cousin and several members of the family before him, was highly extravagant and quite unable to live within his means. He had remained in England at Leeds Castle and in 1746 married for the second time another heiress, Dorothy Sarah Best, the daughter of a Kentish brewer. This marriage replenished his coffers for a while. However, leopards do not change their spots and once again he found himself in financial difficulties. So in desperation both he and George William turned to Lord Fairfax for help. Reluctantly, and doubtless after many a lecture on their fecklessness, he finally came to their rescue, but it was to be the last time they received his largesse.

The late 1760s proved to be the end of an era for the Fairfax family and indeed it also marked the closing stages of a golden era for Colonial Virginia. Although change was in the air, life carried on much as before for the Fairfax's at Belvoir, hunting and roistering with their neighbours and relations, not least among them George Washington. Following the death of Lawrence Washington in 1752, his widow Anne, Colonel William Fairfax's daughter, had passed the plantation of Mount Vernon to George and remarried to a member of the Lee family. It was at this time that we encounter another member of the Fairfax family for the first time, Bryan, the younger surviving half-brother of George William. Bryan, later the 8th Lord Fairfax, would become a very close friend of the future President and would one day be a pall bearer at his funeral – a clear sign of their mutual esteem. But all that was in the future and for now they hunted and made merry. The friendship they formed during these years would be strong enough to survive the turmoil of the years ahead.

7. The Virginian Exiles

In 1771 Robert Fairfax bade farewell to his brother for the last time and returned to England. He never did learn to control his finances, despite his brother Lord Fairfax's generosity and his previous marriage to two heiresses. In 1778 Robert spent large sums refurbishing the reception rooms of Leeds Castle for a brief visit by King George III and his wife Queen Charlotte who were inspecting the army encamped nearly. As a result of this and other extravagances, he would spend his final years in near poverty, in sharp contrast to his frugal brother in America.

Two years later in 1773 George William and his wife Sally made the decision to return to England. The matter of his uncle's inheritance was still unsettled and with his prospects no brighter in Virginia, another voyage to England seemed his best option. Perhaps he also saw that the growing anger and resentment of the colonists against high-handed British rule would only end in tears. If so his decision was certainly very prescient.

The voyage to England was not something that anyone would undertake lightly: it was long, arduous and ships frequently foundered *en route*. So it is not surprising to learn that before setting off, George William sought prayers for a safe journey from the Reverend Lee Massey and his congregation at Pohick Church, Occoquan, near Belvoir. This was after all an age when death could come swiftly and in unexpected ways. It certainly made for God-fearing people, and the clergy were held in high esteem. To illustrate this point a fascinating exchange of letters between George William and Mr Lee Massey dated 4th July 1773 has come down to us. It reads as follows:

> *'Mr and Mrs Fairfax's most respectful compliments wait on Mr Massey. They beg the favour of him to desire the*

prayers of the Congregation, this day, to Almighty God for a safe and happy passage to some persons shortly intending to go to sea.'

The Reverend Mr Massey's reply was not entirely what the Fairfax's might have expected although it was friendly enough and speaks of a close friendship between the two parties:

'I received your ticket at Church, but forebore to comply with your request, because such a compliance would exceed my commission. I am authorised to call on the Congregation to pray for persons distressed either in mind, body, or estate, but have no right to vary from the public liturgy to adapt it in new cases, without the sanction of public authority, which (I believe) is never granted for private purposes, but only in cases where the public are concerned, and then a form of prayers is composed and enjoined for the purpose. However, though I cannot demand the prayer of the people for you before you embark, yet, when you are at sea…if my own private prayers can be of any avail, you have them unfeignedly – not only that you and Mrs Fairfax may arrive safely in Britain, but you may succeed in every other lawful undertaking, be healthy during life, and happy forever.

I am, respectfully sir, Your most humble servant, Lee Massey.'

Their departure was obviously sad for those they left behind, not least their good friends George and Martha Washington, who, as Washington notes in his journal, came to see them off: '*Mrs Washington and self went to Belvoir to see them take ship.*' Had they known it would be the last they would ever see of one another, it would have been an even sadder occasion.

Happily, the voyage passed without incident, although it has been said that as their ship sailed up the Thames it passed another vessel outward bound for Boston, laden with a certain cargo of tea that would change the world for ever, not least for George William and the Fairfax family.

Safely in England, George William set about resolving the dispute over his Yorkshire estates once and for all. A settlement was finally agreed and his future welfare assured, but there would be no return voyage to Virginia. The glowing embers that had smouldered in the hearts and minds of the colonists for so many years finally burst into flame in 1775. The Revolution had begun!

Whether George William actually wanted to return to Virginia we cannot say, but whatever the case, the war certainly forced his hand. Apart from the sheer impracticality of returning home to Virginia during a war, there were other reasons too. His relationship with the old Proprietor and his cousin Thomas Martin had been poor for some time and his prospects in Virginia had been stymied at every turn. So whatever the outcome of the rebellion, which in the early stages looked likely to be bad for the rebels, life in England would certainly be a great deal safer. Perhaps the truth was that George William never really felt at home in the New World despite the comfort and relative safety of life at Belvoir. After all, he had visited England often and now had some financial security from his uncle's inheritance to provide for his and his wife's welfare. This was important as the war put a stop to any remittances from Virginia, which might have left them in dire straits. As he says in a letter to a friend John Norton discussing the prospects for peace in 1776:

> *'I cannot believe that the Ministry will be able to get 50,000 men landed in America, or that the Commissioners will do any thing effectual, unless they are allowed to treat with the Continental Congress. They may indeed protract matters, and enrich themselves with the overflowing of your T___Y (taxes), but I expect very little national advantage from their negotiations. However I do sincerely and most heartily wish, that I may be*

> *disappointed, and that the Commissioners may obtain peace and tranquility throughout the British Dominions, tho' from letters lately received from George Washington, I must agree with you, there is very little prospect of so happy an event. Sad reflections for me, my good Sir, whose chief resources are now cut off, and forced to contract his living to the small income he has here.'*

Despite this, George William and Sally were still able to provide financial assistance to American prisoners of war held in England, something that did not go unnoticed in America either. When in 1780 Washington heard the Virginia Legislature was planning to confiscate George William's property, he swiftly wrote to Fairfax's agent Robert Carter Nicholas:

> *'I hope, I trust, that no act of Legislation has affected, or can affect, the property of this Gentnr. Otherwise than in common with every good, and well disposed Citizen of America. It is a well known fact that his departure for England was not only antecedent to the present rupture with England, but before there was the most distant prospect of a serious dispute with that Country, and if it is necessary to adduce proof of his attachment to the interests of America since his residence there and of the aid he has given to many of our distressed Countrymen in that Kingdom, abundant instances may be adduced, not only by the Gentnr alluded to in his letter of Dec 5, 1779, but by others that are known to me, and on whom justice to Colo. Fairfax will make it necessary to call if occasion should require the facts to be ascerted.'*

This letter certainly seems to have done the trick and George William's property was spared seizure, eventually passing to his nephew Ferdinando Fairfax on his death.

This is not to say George William's action was without risk. Indeed, his open support for American prisoners and the Rebellion itself put him in great danger, as we discover from a remarkable letter he wrote to Washington after hostilities had ceased:

> *'Permit me, altho' an humble individual, and unfortunately out of the way of contributing any mite to the great, the glorious cause of Liberty, to offer my best thanks for all your Exertions, disinterested perseverance to the End of the great work...I glory in calling myself an American...During the war I frequently did myself the honour of Addressing a line to you, some of which I hope kiss'd your hand, others were I know intercepted, and sent to the Minister, one of which had like to have cost me dear, but happily for me, I was related to a Lady, whose interest at Court saved me from persecution. I every moment expected a messenger to take me into Custody. Indeed my dear Sir, I have been in a very disagreeable Situation, was obliged to leave Yorkshire to get out of the way of being informed against by some Relations, who I apprehended, would have hung me to get my little Estate joining to theirs, but I thank Heaven, you and our brave countrymen, times are much altered and I am now as much Courted as I was before despised as an American...It is not possible for you to conceive how I am pestered, by applications, for Letters of Introduction to your Excellency: and other Persons of consequence in Virginia, by men, that would, twelve months ago, have thought it a reflection upon them to be even seen in my company.'*

Washington clearly missed his old friends very much and never let an opportunity pass to suggest they return home - as we see in his reply, writing that he lived in hope of *'seeing you and Mrs Fairfax once more the Inhabitants of Belvoir, and greeting you both there, the intimate companions of our old Age as you have been of our younger years.'*

Whether they ever considered returning we cannot tell, but when Belvoir tragically burnt to the ground in 1783 they must have realised there was no going back. The Virginian exiles would spend their remaining years far from Belvoir, and far from their family and friends. In 1784 they acquired a lease on Writhlington Manor, near the fashionable spa town of Bath in the west of England, where society would gather to take the waters and gamble. Although the house is no longer standing, it is said to have been remarkably similar in size and style to Belvoir.

Despite the distance between them, the letters continued to flow and in the same year we find Washington writing to George William requesting he find him a 'knowing farmer – with his assistance and advice I shall be able to dispense with a steward.' Fairfax duly sent him one James Bloxham, although this was not a success as Mr Bloxham turned out to be inefficient and lazy.

Rather more successful was the gift of seeds that Sally sent to Washington at Mount Vernon from her garden at Writhlington, as we see in a letter George William writes on her behalf.

> *'Mrs Fairfax bids me to say she will take care to send the seeds of many kinds of shrubs that she thinks is not in Virginia...and when your hothouse is ready to receive the plants we will send you many of the myrtles and geraniums...you know a flower was ever Mrs Fairfax's hobby.'*

This obviously meant the world to Washington who is delighted to hear of the gift he is soon receive and writes in reply:

> *'I will receive with great pleasure and gratitude the seeds of any trees or shrubs which are not natives of this country, but reconcilable to the climate of it, that she may be so obliging as to send me; and while my attentions are bestowed on the nurture of them, it would, if anything was necessary to do it, remind me of the happy moments I have spent on this and other subjects with that lady at Belvoir.'*

So here they lived quietly and frugally for what remained of George William's life. That life, so bright with early promise, had been full of disappointments: passed over for preferment in Virginia, he had lost his beautiful home on the Potomac and to cap it all, when Lord Fairfax finally died in 1781, he was left nothing in his will, 'Not even a mourning ring', as George William put it. Nor did he inherit the title of Lord Fairfax as he had once expected. He died aged 61 in 1787 and was buried in the little church of St Mary Magdalene, Writhlington, where he was later joined by his wife Sally, who outlived him by twenty-four years.

Despite all this, Sally always stood by her husband, as we see when she writes to George William's sister in 1788 defending his reputation:

> 'Weeping has robbed me of sight...your dear brother was as highly esteemed as any man in England. As a proof of it I now send you what appeared in the London papers at the time of his decease.'

However, we later see her true feelings when she writes bitterly:

> 'Thank God, I have outlived those prejudices of education and know that the worthy man is to be preferred to the high born who has not merit to recommend him.' If only she had married the man who had truly loved her, the 'worthy' George Washington and not the 'high born' George William Fairfax...but of course age and circumstance had conspired against them.

After her husband's death Sally gave up the lease on Writhlington Manor and spent her years of widowhood in Bath at No. 9 Lansdown Place East, a fine example of Georgian architecture that remains entirely unchanged today. How sad to think that Sally, so beautiful and admired in her youth, would have to endure such a lonely old age, so far from her homeland and friends, not least her old admirer, now so famous as the First President.

Washington never forgot Sally and shortly before his death he wrote touchingly to Sally one more time. Now at last there was no concealing his true feelings for her:

> *'During the past five and twenty years...so many important events have occurred, and such changes in men and things have taken place, as the compass of a letter would give you but an inadequate idea of. None of which events, however, nor all of them together have been able to eradicate from my mind the recollection of those happy moments, the happiest of my life, which I have enjoyed in your company.'*

What an admission from the Father of the Nation! More to the point, had he not been happily married to the dependable Martha for all those years? So perhaps we should treat these words as the outpourings of a tired old man, yearning for his youth. But what sweet and charming words they are! They are still moving over two hundred years after they were written. How consoling they must have been to poor lonely Sally then.

In 1978 the Church of St Mary Magdalene was deconsecrated and the memorial plaque to this Virginian couple was taken to Claverton Manor in Bath, the home of the American Museum in Britain. Today visitors to the Museum can wander through a re-creation of the rose garden at Mount Vernon and in a bower beneath the wall will see the elegant plaque bearing these words to George William and his wife, called 'Sarah' here but better known to us as 'Sally':

To the Memory of the Honourable
GEORGE WILLIAM FAIRFAX
Of Towlston in Yorkshire
Who died on the 3rd April 1787
Aged 61 Years
And of Sarah his Wife

Given the life-long affection that George Washington had for Sally this seems an entirely appropriate resting place for their memorial.

The Manor is long gone and the church is now used as a private home. In the summer of 2011 I visited Writhlington and was shown the site of the Manor. Some remains of the outbuildings can be seen and the ancient yews and box trees are evidence of its former majesty. A little further from the house down a quiet country lane lies a stone pillar, largely forgotten and buried amongst the undergrowth, recording the presence of these two Virginian exiles long ago and a very long way from that majestic house on the Potomac that was their home.

And what of their beloved Belvoir, that elegant mansion above the Potomac, built by Colonel William with such care and attention, and the scene of so much merriment? Its sad fate was as follows.

When George William Fairfax left Belvoir for England in 1773, the estate was rented to the Revd Andrew Morton for seven years, and in 1774 the furnishings were sold at auction. The sale was arranged by George Washington who had power of attorney over his old friends' affairs, which Washington refers to in a letter to Bryan Fairfax. Washington himself was one of the larger purchasers at the sale, spending a total of £169, 12 shillings and 6 pence for a variety of items including beds, carpets, looking glasses, 'a Mahogy chest & drawers in Mrs F's chamber' (still at Mount Vernon), chairs, 'Curtains from the dining room', 2 candlesticks, 'a bust of the immortal Shakespeare and a 'Mahogy card table'. Perhaps the presence of his friends' furniture was some consolation for their absence?

Then in 1783 tragedy struck when Belvoir was burnt to the ground in a devastating fire. As Washington lamented in a letter of 1785 to George William in England:

'But alas! Belvoir is no more! I took a ride there the other day to visit the ruins – and ruins indeed they are. The dwelling house and the two brick buildings in front underwent the ravages of the fire: the walls of which are much injured: the other houses are sinking under the depredation of time and inattention and I believe are now scarcely worth repairing. In a word, the whole are, or very soon will be a heap of ruin. When I viewed them – when I considered the happiest moments of my life had been spent there, when I could not trace a room in the house (now all rubbish) that did not bring to my mind the recollection of pleasing scenes: I was obliged to fly from them and came home with painful sensations and sorrowing for the contrast.'

George William wrote in reply:

'Your pathetic description of the Ruin of Belvoir House produced many tears and sighs from the former Mistress of it, tho' at first hearing of the Fire, she felt no shock.'

Right up to the very end of his life Washington still clung onto those cherished memories of Sally at Belvoir, as we see from a letter he wrote to her in May 1798:

'And it is a matter of some regret, when I cast my eyes towards Belvoir, which I often do, to reflect that the former Inhabitants of it, with whom we lived in such harmony and friendship, no longer reside there: and that the ruins can only be viewed as the momento of former pleasures.'

Ferdinando Fairfax, George William's nephew and heir, inherited the plantation and lived for a while in a small dwelling near the creek, known as the White House. The bluffs below the former mansion site were quarried for building stone, but the house itself was left in ruin.

Further devastation befell Belvoir during the War of 1812-14 between Britain and the United Sates. In August 1814, after the British had attacked and burned Washington, their fleet was bombarded by American guns positioned high on the bluffs of Belvoir as they made their escape down the Potomac. This minor engagement is known confusingly as the Battle of the White House, in reference to the White House at Belvoir, not the more famous one in Washington. Actually, the Executive Mansion was at that time of bare brick. It was burned by the British Army in the same year and only became white when it was painted after the war to hide the scorch marks.

The Fairfax family's association with Belvoir ended with the death of Ferdinando Fairfax in 1820 and after passing through several hands it finally became an army base in 1917, which it remains to this day.

Such was the sad fate that befell this magnificent symbol of the Fairfax family's former power and glory in Colonial Virginia. William Fairfax and his second wife Deborah are buried there and there is a memorial in the grounds to two of their sons.

All trace of Belvoir in its heyday has not been entirely lost: on the lawn in front of Leeds Castle there is a sundial and if you look very carefully you will see the name 'Belvoir' inscribed upon it. On a sunny day it will tell you the time there, just as it did over two hundred years ago, a poignant memorial to that golden age when the Fairfax family held sway over both Leeds Castle in Kent and Belvoir in Virginia.

8. The End of the Northern Neck Proprietary

When the war broke out in 1775, Lord Fairfax was 82 years old. He was far too old to have any influence on one side or the other, but he did find himself in rather an awkward situation. He owed his position and the ownership of the Proprietary to the Crown, although as a long-time resident of Virginia and close friend of many of the chief rebels, not least Washington himself, he almost certainly felt a closer affinity to them. However, with his brother Robert at Leeds Castle and George William in Bath, not to mention his Martin relations, he had to tread very carefully, lest he jeopardise their positions. So as his long life slowly drew to an end, he lived out his remaining days quietly at Greenway Court unmolested and largely ignored while the war raged around him.

When Lord Cornwallis surrendered at Yorktown on 19th October 1781 it marked the end of British Colonial rule and the birth of the United States of America. It also marked the end for Lord Fairfax. It is said that upon hearing the news of the British defeat, Lord Fairfax called out to his old retainer: *'Come Joe, carry me to bed! for I'm sure 'tis time for me to go hence!'* And sure enough on 7th December 1781, Lord Fairfax was carried away to that great hunting ground in the sky. He was eighty-eight, a quite remarkable age for the time.

Lord Fairfax was greatly respected and his passing was mourned by many, not least his old friend and former apprentice, George Washington. Although now the commander of the Revolutionary forces, when news came to him of the old Lord's death, he still found time to write these heartfelt words: *'Although the good old Lord lived to an advanced age I feel concern at his death.'* Amen to that.

He was buried within the communion rail in Winchester's former Frederick Parish Church. However, in 1829 the church was raised and his remains were transferred to the new Christ Church at the corner of Washington and Boscawen Streets.

An interesting tale is told about those remains. With the passing of the years the church was enlarged and his tomb forgotten. Then in 1925 more work was begun and a search for his remains was made. At first nothing could be found until a workman, a part-time preacher, dreamed that Lord Fairfax's bones rested in a certain spot. He dug there and, lo and behold, there was the Old Lord. His grave is now located in the side yard of the church.

The oval silver plate from his coffin was for many years in the possession of the Historical Society of Pennsylvania. It had probably been dug up and then removed by a passing Union soldier during the Civil War. This too is now safely back at Christ Church.

One final and rather poignant story remains to be told of Thomas the 6th Lord. Approximately one hundred years after his death, workmen were repairing the roof at another old Fairfax property, Ash Grove, near Tyson's Corner in Fairfax County, when they came across a bundle of dusty and faded parchments in the attic. Among these was a document that told the sad tale of the young Lord's thwarted love for a lady in the heady days of his youth. For this was the very marriage contract drawn up between Lord Fairfax and the young lady who turned him down, preferring 'the higher honour of being a duchess'. It is said that this broke his heart, and as the romantics have it, drove him to his lonely Virginian exile. And the young lady's name? Sadly, we shall never know as the distraught young Lord had carefully cut her name out of the parchment. Evidently the scars of this injustice were slow to heal, if indeed they ever did.

So how can we summarise Lord Fairfax's achievements and legacy? As a young man he had inherited a near hopeless situation from his spendthrift father. The family was

The End of the Northern Neck Proprietary

deeply in debt and had been forced to sell its ancestral estates in Yorkshire. They still owned Leeds Castle in Kent, which had come into the family by way of marriage from the Culpepers, but this was more a costly white elephant than a valuable asset. Then there was the Northern Neck Proprietary far away in Virginia. While this might appear to us a great asset, it had always been plagued with problems and the family were entirely dependent upon the trustworthiness of their agent in the colony. To say that their long-time agent Robert 'King' Carter had failed in this duty would be quite an understatement. He had made himself immensely rich at their expense and thanks to his cavalier behaviour, the Virginia Assembly had openly challenged the very legitimacy of the Proprietary in the courts in 1733. The ensuing litigation dragged on for eleven long years and when it was eventually resolved in his favour, Lord Fairfax had taken the radical step of moving to Virginia. Here he settled in the remote Shenandoah Valley, where he lived a simple homespun life administering the Proprietary himself. Over the next twenty-five years he succeeded in opening up this vast swathe of territory for settlement, but perhaps his greatest legacy was the role he played in educating and training the young George Washington, whom he had employed as a surveyor and who shared his hard life on the frontier.

Through his single-minded stewardship of the Northern Neck Proprietary he had also made himself immensely rich and had he wished, he could have settled his wealth on his Fairfax cousins, but he chose not to do so. His financial legacy was a staggering £47,377, 3 shillings and 9 pence, carefully hoarded in a metal trunk under his bed. (Of this £9,510, 13 shillings and 9 pence was paid in taxes to Mr Milton, the Sheriff.) Apart from his colossal landholdings, his will mentions quantities of gold, silver, plate, china, glass, furniture, books, clothing, kitchen utensils, tools, tack and wagons and sadly, a large number of slaves.

Some experts have reckoned that in today's terms the cash alone would be worth around £350 million ($430 million) and when one considers the dire situation he had inherited from his father, and the early years of financial stricture, his was surely a remarkable achievement. However, it seems he had little interest in this fortune other than as the evidence of a dutiful life. It certainly brought no benefit to the Fairfax family.

So what became of this huge financial legacy and the vast acreage of the Northern Neck Proprietary? Although the title passed to his brother Robert, by then an elderly, down-at-heel widower living at Leeds Castle in England, the only money he received from his brother was a paltry £500 – as the will states 'a considerable pecuniary legacy bequeathed to him by will now cancelled.' There would be no more for the spendthrift Robert.

To his cousin George William, who once dreamed of inheriting both the title and Lord Fairfax's vast property, there was nothing, not even a 'mourning ring' as he bitterly put it. There were various small legacies to his other nieces and nephews, as well as life time annuities to the younger members. As for the bulk of his fortune, this went to his nephew the Reverend Denny Martin, the son of his favourite sister Frances, and many would say that was quite right given the fecklessness of his Fairfax relations.

As for the Proprietary itself, the largest part of this initially went to his brother Robert, now the 7th Lord Fairfax, with a 1/6th share going to his nephew the Reverend Denny Martin. Additionally, Robert was awarded £13,758 in 1792 by Parliament under the terms of the Act for the Relief of American Loyalists, but this was of little use to him as he died shortly afterwards in 1793 and the windfall was promptly swallowed up by his rapacious creditors.

Robert's majority share in the Proprietary then passed to the Reverend Denny, to add to 1/6th interest he had already

The End of the Northern Neck Proprietary

received in Lord Fairfax's will. The one proviso was that his heir should 'procure an Act of Parliament to take upon him the name of Fairfax and coat of arms.' This he duly did, but by Royal Licence, adding the name of Fairfax to his own.

Of course, the will's provisions had little bearing on reality, as the careful plans Lord Fairfax had made for the Proprietary were thwarted by the Revolution. In 1779, a law was passed whereby all Virginian property belonging to British subjects became vested in the Commonwealth of Virginia. Then in 1782 Virginia's General Assembly passed a further Act, sequestering all past and future quit rents. This would have been a disaster for Lord Fairfax's heirs and all his work would have been in vain: however, the Northern Neck was later exempted, an acknowledgement of the Fairfax family's loyalty to the cause of the rebels. Doubtless the Fairfax family's close friendship with the First President also played no small part in this either.

None of this made plain sailing for Denny Martin and the Proprietary. As frequently happens in the wake of revolutions, chaos ensued. Although the Treaty of Paris in 1783 brought some order to the situation, Denny soon found himself embroiled in litigation with the Virginia Assembly over the status of the Proprietary which would drag on for many long years.

Finally, he had enough and in 1794 the exasperated Denny accepted an offer from a syndicate consisting of his lawyer John Marshall, his brother James Markham Marshall and Raleigh Colston to buy out the Martins' residual interest in the Northern Neck for £20,000.

Incidentally, the Manor of Leeds, some 160,382 acres surrounding Lord Fairfax's Greenway Court, which had been excluded from the sale to the Marshall syndicate, was eventually sold to the same syndicate of Virginians for £14,000 in 1806.

So as we can see, it was Lord Fairfax's Martin relations who came out on top after his death, although their enjoyment of his fortune would be brief. Denny's brother Thomas Bryan Martin, who had become agent to Lord Fairfax in 1751, was given 8,840 acres of land as well as Greenway Court. Upon his death in 1798, he left Greenway Court and 1,000 acres to his housekeeper Betsy Powers, while the remaining land was sold for the benefit of his three sisters Frances, Sybilla and Anna Susanna. The nearby town of Martinsburg was named in his honour and a monument was erected to his memory when it was laid out in 1778 by Colonel Adam Stephen.

The final member of the Martin family to benefit from Lord Fairfax's estate was the youngest of the brothers, Philip, the last leaf on the tree. A career soldier and lifelong bachelor, he had the 'cock' of his hat shot off by a 26lb ball at the siege of Gibraltar, later rising to the rank of Major General in the British army. When his brother Denny died in 1800, he inherited Leeds Castle where he lived with his three unmarried sisters until his death in 1821, at the grand old age of eighty-eight.

The inheritance left Philip an immensely wealthy man but without any kind of heir he faced a great dilemma. Who would inherit Leeds Castle and his great fortune? As a practical military man, Philip decided to look for an heir from among the Wykeham family, who were very distant relations of his father. The lucky recipient was to be Fiennes Wykeham, and distantly related he certainly was: he was the great-grandson of the half-sister of General Martin's grandfather's half-sister on his father's side! In addition to Leeds Castle, the lucky Mr Wykeham also received the residue of General Martin's Virginian legacy, the then very considerable sum of £30,000.

The only condition was that Fiennes Wykeham should assume the name and coat of arms of the Martin family and

The End of the Northern Neck Proprietary

this is how Leeds Castle passed from the Culpeper, Fairfax and Martin families to the newly created family of Wykeham-Martin. It would remain in their hands until 1926 when it was sold to the rich American heiress Mrs Olive Filmer–Wilson, later Lady Baillie after her marriage to Sir Adrian Baillie in 1933. Lady Baillie had found the castle in a state of total disrepair and it is entirely due to her munificence that it is in such fine condition today. Since her death in 1974, the castle has been administered by a charitable trust, the Leeds Castle Foundation.

So here it is that we reach the end of the long saga of the Northern Neck Proprietary of Virginia, which began with its creation in 1649 by King Charles II and the families who were its Proprietors: the Culpepers, Fairfax's and Martins.

This is not the end of the story, but it does mark the end of a golden era for the Fairfax family when they held sway over countless acres of Northern Virginia and exerted real influence over the people and events of their extraordinary time. Never again would they have the position and prestige enjoyed by the 6th Lord, but that is not to say their subsequent history is any the less interesting

9. Bryan Fairfax, 8th Lord Fairfax: A lifetime of change

If you take a look at the line of descent of many of the great English titles you will find that it has often been quite tortuous and convoluted. Those of the Dukes of Norfolk or Westminster are good examples, where quite distant cousins have inherited the title when the previous Duke died without a male heir. So it was with the Fairfax family. When Robert the 7th Lord Fairfax died in 1793, he too was childless. So we have to go back to an earlier holder of the title to find a descendant who would be next in line.

The father of the 6th and 7th Lords, Thomas 5th Lord Fairfax, had a younger brother Henry and it was his grandson who would became the next Lord Fairfax. Colonel William Fairfax of Belvoir was Henry's eldest son, so on Robert's death in 1793 his only surviving son Bryan became the 8th Lord Fairfax.

By this time the United States of America was firmly established with its own constitution and its existing borders defined, at least for now. Those who had fought against its birth had either fled or were dead. Titles were out of place in the new republic and Bryan accepted this state of affairs, being happy to be known simply as 'the Reverend Bryan Fairfax' after his ordination into the Episcopal Church in 1789. He obviously saw no point in drawing attention to his noble birth, with its association to the old order and it was only at the very end of his life that he made the long journey to England to lay claim to the title in 1798. Why he took the trouble to do this is unclear, but maybe he felt it was his duty to establish the right of his son and any later descendants.

The position of the Fairfax's had been decidedly awkward during the turmoil of the Revolution, not least as the Northern Neck Proprietary was a gift of the Crown and the 6th Lord was de facto a member of the House of Lords. However, the family and their individual land holdings were left unmolested throughout the years of conflict. Much of this had to do with the First President's respect for old Lord Fairfax, although he was not the only member of the Fairfax family to whom he was close. Of course, the life-long flame he carried for Sally Cary Fairfax is well known, but what is perhaps more surprising was the lasting friendship with her husband George William. Although exiled in England since 1773, they were still in regular correspondence right up until George William's death in 1787. However, the member of the family perhaps closest to the President was Bryan, especially after the deaths of Lord Fairfax and George William Fairfax, and now the only link with those halcyon days of hunting and merry making at Belvoir.

Born only four years apart, Washington and Fairfax had grown up as neighbours and would regularly ride to hounds as young men. Although their careers and political opinions would come to differ widely, they maintained a close friendship through thick and thin. The evidence for this is the considerable number of letters they wrote to one another throughout their lives, even in the darkest and most dangerous days of the Revolutionary War.

We owe our knowledge of these letters to the scholarship of Donald M. Sweig and Elizabeth S. David in their book *A Fairfax Friendship - The Complete Correspondence Between George Washington and Bryan Fairfax 1754-1799* published in 1982. This excellent catalogue of their correspondence with its erudite commentary has been invaluable and I am extremely grateful to them for their diligence.

These letters concern all kinds of subject from shared domestic matters to religion and most importantly their differing political views. What emerges is a character portrait of both men and a window on their world before, during, and after the Revolutionary War. George, the strong minded military leader, soon to be father of the new nation, and Bryan, the hesitant and somewhat indecisive mystic, torn by his loyalty to the old order and the Crown but equally loyal to his Virginian friends.

George Washington's life and his remarkable achievements are minutely recorded and known to all, and he is justly regarded as one of the great figures in history alongside Julius Caesar, Napoleon Bonaparte and Alexander the Great. Bryan Fairfax by contrast has what can only be described as a 'walk on' part, although during their lifetime it is clear they held each other in mutual respect and friendship. However, to a student of the Fairfax family history he is nonetheless important, not least for this close relationship with one of the giants of history.

Bryan was born in 1737 at Belvoir but unlike most children of the ruling class, most notably his half-brother George William, he had not been sent to England to be educated, but instead went to live with his mother's family, the Clarkes, in Massachusetts. His uncle John Clarke had established himself as a merchant in Barbados and so, in 1752 the 16 year-old Bryan was sent there to learn the business. Of course, in those benighted times, an important part of their business would have included slave trading, but, I am happy to note, Bryan found it abhorrent and he was soon back in Virginia.

With the outbreak of the French & Indian War in 1755 Bryan was commissioned as a lieutenant in Captain George Mercer's Company of Militia stationed at Fort Cumberland. He served there under his young friend George Washington. It was at this time that Bryan had the first of the religious experiences that would one day lead to his taking holy orders. While on sentry duty from midnight to two, the most dangerous watch, he sent his fellow sentry away and, *'As soon as I was alone, I kneeled down and determined not to rise but to continue crying and wrestling with God until he had mercy on me.'* Whether he was punished for this dereliction of duty we do not know, but it was certainly an epiphany for the young cadet.

Then, in 1757 he suddenly resigned his commission in a fit of pique, without telling his father and set off to join the 'Northern Regulars' under an assumed name. His reason appears to have been an unrequited love. On leave he had attended 'Several merry meetings and dancing in Westmoreland and Essex in the course of which he had 'addressed' a young lady, who to his chagrin rebuffed him. Having got as far as Annapolis, his brother-in-law John Carlyle's wise counsel persuaded the hot headed young man to return home where he was briefly commissioned as a captain in the Fairfax Militia.

Bryan was clearly not cut out for soldiering, but did it really matter? His position at the peak of colonial Virginian society had been clear from the start: at an early age his father Colonel William had given him several land grants of approximately 5,000 acres and on his death in 1757, he received another 5,000. When his courageous brother William Henry was killed at Quebec in 1759 he received further acreages, approximately doubling his landholdings. Then in 1765 Lord Fairfax gave him the Manor of Great Falls in Fairfax County, which totalled another 12,588 acres. He was now a major landowner with approximately 30,000 acres to his name and all the prestige they brought. As Jane Austen would famously put it in *Pride and Prejudice*: '*It is a truth universally acknowledged, that a single man in possession of a good fortune, must be in want of a wife*' and so it was for Bryan, who in 1759 married Elizabeth Cary, the younger sister of the vivacious Sally Cary Fairfax, the wife of his half-brother George William.

He now set about building a house for his wife on his Great Falls property which he named Towlston Grange after a Fairfax house in Yorkshire. It took several years to build and it was not until 1767 that they were able to move in, so in the meantime they continued to live at Belvoir. Meanwhile, in 1761 he had rented Greenhill, a nearby farm of 197 acres and there their first two children were born. He was appointed a justice of the peace in 1759 and this, together with the management of his wide acres, kept him busy when not hunting to hounds with friends such as George Washington.

As we have already seen Bryan was a restless man and throughout his life he would constantly change course. An exchange of letters between his brother-in-law John Carlyle and George William in England makes this point clearly.

> *'Your brother Mr B. Fairfax is much altered, and is quite tired of Tolston for want of company. He is determined to take a house and lot in this town (Alexandria), but Colonel George Lee put him out by telling him it would cost him £200 per annum. Now he is falled upon another scheame. You must remember a little house Mr Green bought on M. Green's land, and your brother has taken a lease of that place for his life and is about scantlings, making bricks and is to be living there next spring…His utmost wish was to be settled at Towlston, and now he would not live there for the world.'*

To which George William replied in exasperation: 'He soon tires of anywhere.'

Although Bryan was clearly a difficult fellow and given to sudden changes of heart, he and his wife Elizabeth produced four children, Thomas, later the 9th Lord Fairfax, Sally, Billy, (who would die as an infant) and Ferdinando.

The most interesting member of this family was little Sally. Although she would die tragically young aged only nineteen, during her brief life she played an important role within the family, particularly during her father's extended absences. That apart, there would be little to say about her but for a remarkable stroke of luck; Sally had kept a diary and childish though it may have been, it survived and was written up by a later member of the family, the celebrated author Constance Burton Harrison (1843 -1920), a granddaughter of Thomas 9th Lord Fairfax. Cousin Constance, as I shall call her, entitled her story 'A Little Centennial Lady' when it was published in Scribner's monthly magazine in 1876. Through Sally's charming and keenly observed notes, we can glimpse a fleeting picture of life at Towlston before the Revolution, as seen through the eyes of this bright young child.

It begins in 1771 when Sally could have been no more than eight or nine, with the family preparing for a Christmas Ball:

'On Thursday, 26th of decem. mama made 6 mince pyes and 7 custards 12 tarts, 1 chicking pye and 4 pudings for the ball.

Miss molly payne, and mr perce baillis and mr William Payn and Mr William Sandford, Mr Moody and Miss Jenny, a man who lives at Colchester, Mr hurst, Mrs Hursts husband, young harry gunnell, a son of old William gunnell john scot from the little falls, Mr Watts and Mr Hunter these are all the gentlemen and ladies that were at the ball. Mrs Gunnell brought her sucking child with her.

On Satterday the 28th Decem. I won 10 shillings of Mr Wm. Payne at chess.'

Sally was obviously a very smart young lady.

She continues:

'On Monday night, when papa was at Mount Vernon my aunt Fairfax sent my muslin apron to him which she gave me when I was at Belvoir, but I did not bring it home with me so she made miss Polly work it for me and sent it to mount Vernon for p. to bring to me which he did and in it she sent me a note. The apron is worked mighty pretty – peter gullch and Nicholas money all came for money.

> *On Friday the 3rd jan. came jonn vain to undertake the building of the hen-house. He got no encouragement so he went away the same way he came.*
>
> *On Friday the 3rd jan. came here granny. she cut me out a short gown, and stayed all night.*
>
> *On Friday 3 of january papa went to collo. Washington's and came home again the next Wednesday which was the 8th.'*

Sally was no shrinking violet either as we see from an outburst of anger at the cruel treatment of a favourite cat:

> 'On friday the 3 jan. that vile man adam at night kild a poor cat of rage because she eat a bit of meat out of his hand and scratched it. O vile wreach of new negrows if he was mine I woud cut him to pieces a son of a gun a nice negrow he shued be kild himself by rites.'

Sally never seemed to miss a trick and kept a careful eye of domestic matters too:

> 'On Thursday, 2nd of Jan Margory went to washing and brought all the things in ready done on Thursday the 9th of the same month I think she was a great while about them a wole week if you will believe me reader.
>
> *On Saturday the 11 of jan. I made a card box to put my necklasses in and I put them in.*
>
> *On Saturday 11of jan. papa measured me as you come out of the chamber.*
>
> *On Monday the 13 of jan mamma made some tea for a wonder indeed.'*

Tea was at that time rare and very expensive.

> 'On Thursday the 16th Jan. there came a woman and a girl and mama bought 3 old hens from them and gave them

to me which reduced her debt she owed me which was five and ninepence to three and ninepence which she now owes me fiveteen pence about nancy perrys ribbon, which she never paid. ...S...F...X'

Thrifty too!

'On Friday 17th of jan. I mended Tommy's shirt from top to toe.

On Saturday 18th Jan. top came here to see Dolly.

Oh! Little wide-awake, as if the sable sweethearts could elude you!

On Friday the 17th Jan. poor luch colton died of a dropsy 1772 her child is also dead.

On Friday 24th Jan. john Jacson came here and went hunting with papa.

On Friday 24th. about twelve o'clock at night margery was brought to bed a boy 1772.

On Monday the 27th of jan. there fell an amazing snow, two foot and a half, on Tuesday the 28 of jan. I cracked a loaf of sugar. On Tuesday Adam cut down a cherry tree. On Friday the 14 of febberary the red and white cow calfed and had a red and white calf 1772.'

Thus ends the record of a month in an old Virginian house before the Revolution. Sally's bright and busy nature also caught the attention of their neighbour George Washington who speaks of her as 'my dear little humorous Sally.' But all too soon events would sweep away this comfortable and familiar world, ushering in a new air of uncertainty and sorrow for the family at Towlston.

By 1774 the deep resentment felt towards London throughout the Colonies had grown to fever pitch. The

Fairfax Resolves, a set of constitutional demands drawn up by George Mason and George Washington in Fairfax County that would form the basis of the coming revolt, gave flesh to these feelings. The events leading up to this deserve some explanation and involve an event known to every schoolchild, the Boston Tea Party. In 1773, some Bostonians had boarded ships at anchor in the harbour and dumped a large cargo of tea into the water. It was a protest against the highly-resented taxes imposed by the Tea Act of that year. As an act of revenge, the British then imposed the 'Intolerable' or 'Coercive' Act which closed the port of Boston and imposed direct rule from London. Hoping this would isolate the malcontents in Boston, it had exactly the opposite effect, uniting all the colonials in opposition to the British. The Fairfax Resolves, the first Continental Congress and Lexington would follow.

Bryan's friends and neighbours were behind the revolt to a man – Washington's, Lees, Alexanders, Cary's, Amblers, Masons, Nicholas's, Randolphs, Carters, Corbins, Taylors, Nelsons and many more. All were planters of course, men of property and at the peak of society. This is a remarkable fact, as Ron Chernow points out in his Pulitzer winning book, Washington - A Life, since most revolutions are started by those at the bottom of society. The real cause of the planters' fury was initially not some abstract desire to create their own nation but a long-held grievance against their agents in London who took advantage of their position to cheat the planters out of a fair deal. All manufactured goods came from England, right down to the bricks for their houses, which were purchased with the wealth produced by the colonies, chiefly tobacco and cotton. As a result of these sharp practices, most of the planters were deeply in debt to their agents and their sense of great injustice had predictable and fatal consequences.

Fairfax was not exempt from this, in fact he even considered moving to England as a way of alleviating his financial hardship, but he could not bring himself to join in with the revolutionary movement. Perhaps it was his rather otherworldly nature that stopped him, leaving him detached from the turmoil that surrounded him. Throughout all this, his friendship with Washington never weakened or failed. Perhaps Washington realised that his old friend posed no threat to their plans so he was left alone, sadly contemplating the end of the old order.

This did not stop Fairfax from trying to intercede between the warring factions, and in an effort to persuade his old friend not to break all ties with England, he wrote to Washington in this vein. The reply he received was polite but to the point:

'Dear Sir,

John has just delivered to me your favor of yesterday, which I shall be obliged to answer in a more concise manner, than I could wish, as I am very much engaged in raising one of the additions to my house, which I think (perhaps it is fancy) goes on better whilst I am present, than in my absence from the workmen.

I own to you, Sir, I wished much to hear of your making an open declaration of taking a poll for this county, upon Colonel West's publicly declining last Sunday; and I should have written to you on the subject, but for information then received from several gentlemen in the churchyard, of your having refused to do so, for the reasons assigned in your letter; upon which, as I think the country never stood more in need of men of abilities and liberal sentiments than now, I entreated several gentlemen at our church yesterday to press Colonel Mason to take a poll, as I really think Major Broadwater, though a good man, might do as well in the discharge of his domestic concerns, as in the capacity of a legislator. And therefore I again express my wish, that either you or Colonel Mason would offer. I can be of little assistance to either, because I early laid it down as a maxim not to propose myself, and solicit for a second.

As to your political sentiments, I would heartily join you in them, so far as relates to a humble and dutiful petition to the throne, provided there was the most distant hope of success. But have we not tried this already? Have we not addressed the Lords, and remonstrated to the Commons? And to what end? Did they deign to look at our petitions? Does it not appear, as clear as the sun in its meridian brightness, that there is a regular, systematic plan formed to fix the right and practice of taxation upon us? Does not the uniform conduct of Parliament for some years past confirm this? Do not all the debates, especially those just brought to us, in the House of Commons on the side of government, expressly declare that America must be taxed in aid of the British funds, and that she has no longer resources within herself? Is there any thing to be expected from petitioning after this? Is not the attack upon the liberty and property of the people of Boston, before restitution of the loss to the India Company was demanded, a plain and self-evident proof of what they are aiming at? Do not the subsequent bills (now I dare say acts), for depriving the Massachusetts Bay of its charter, and for transporting offenders into other colonies or to Great Britain for trial, where it is impossible from the nature of the thing that justice can be obtained, convince us that the administration is determined to stick at nothing to carry its point? Ought we not, then, to put our virtue and fortitude to the severest test?

With you I think it a folly to attempt more than we can execute, as that will not only bring disgrace upon us, but weaken our cause; yet I think we may do more than is generally believed, in respect to the non-importation scheme. As to the withholding of our remittances, that is another point, in which I own I have my doubts on several accounts, but principally on that of justice; for I think, whilst we are accusing others of injustice, we should be just ourselves; and how this can be, whilst we owe a considerable debt, and refuse payment of it to Great

Britain, is to me inconceivable. Nothing but the last extremity, I think, can justify it. Whether this is now come, is the question.

I began with telling you, that I was to write a short letter. My paper informs me I have done otherwise. I shall hope to see you to-morrow, at the meeting of the county in Alexandria, when these points are to be considered.

I am, dear Sir, your most obedient and humble servant.

G. Washington'

This was not the end of Bryan's efforts at conciliation and in 1777 as the war raged, Bryan decided to set out for England in the forlorn hope of bringing the two sides to their senses. It was also all too typical of the impetuous Bryan that he should attempt this with his wife in failing health, leaving the household in the care of the young Sally. Accompanied by his son Thomas, who was destined for a school in England, he got as far as Lancaster, Pennsylvania where he was arrested by the colonists and imprisoned in the common jail for refusing to take the oath of allegiance to the cause. Fortunately help was at hand and he was allowed to go on his way, protected by a pass signed by Washington himself allowing him to proceed 'without hindrance to and from the army'. However, in New York he again fell foul of the authorities for refusing to swear a particularly strong oath of allegiance to the King. Although he was not detained for long he realised his mission was now in tatters, so returned home by way of Washington's camp at Valley Forge.

Despite all the cares weighing upon the young Sally - looking after her sick mother, younger brother and the plantation, she still had time to write to her father in New York. The letter which was recorded by Cousin Constance in an essay of 1888 shows a fairly desperate state of affairs at Towlston:

'Honored Sir:

We last night had the pleasure of your last letter, which we earnestly waited for, and which mama, not being very well to write, has desired me to answer, which I wish you may ever receive for there seems to be a great many things to interfere and prevent its journey. Mama seems very unwilling to a separation of one or two years, at any rate, and desires you will shorten the time as much as you can, which at any rate will sit exceeding heavy on her. She is at present better than she has been. I carried her to Alexandria and she employed a doctor there who prescribed something Beneficial – I wish I could write free and unreserved, for I have many things I would say to my dear and ever beloved father that I don't like the curious should see.

I will endeavour to act in the department I am in as well as circumstances will permit, the exceeding troublesome in some respects, however as to your second son, I think the best way will be to have him inoculated and send him to school, for it does not suit otherwise, and a friend of yours is very ready to board him; if you stay long enough at New York, pray write your pleasure in this regard.

The family here are all as well as can be am glad to hear no more odd adventures befell you in your way. I suppose you met no difficulty where you are, nothing could reconcile me to your voyage but the trust in the Almighty that you will safely return. I suppose you will leave my brother in the other land. Pray do not omit writing and make him do it. 'tis owing to the general's interposition that you will receive this, I am exceeding glad of his protection. Mama will not be able to go to Alexandria again this winter, there is always a regiment of soldiers inoculated there, a'most, and the infection is never out of town. She will be exceeding lonsom this year, however this is circuloctious – I hope to often hear, and yet don't know how. Hon'd Sir give my love to my brother, I hope he will acquire the politer assurance and affable cheerfulness of a gentleman, and yet not forget the incidents of Fairfax County. I must conclude with the family your truly & most affectectedly dutiful Daughter,

S. FAIRFAX'

Sadly this is the last we ever hear of plucky little Sally; she was probably no more than seventeen or eighteen at this time and had been engaged to be married to a member of the Washington family, but alas this was not to be. For poor Sally, her father's favourite and the apple of everyone's eye, would die the next year, a life so brief and so full of promise, yet largely unfulfilled. Cousin Constance tells us that Sally's brother Thomas would always talk fondly about his sister right up until his death in 1846, such was his love for her.

To add to his woes, in the very same year Bryan's wife Elizabeth also passed away, leaving him to cope with the family on his own. This state of affairs did not last long and by 1780 he had re-married another Virginian lady, Jane Dennison by whom he had two daughters.

The following year, in a mirror to Bryan's own turmoil, the world was turned upside down. General Washington, not without a little help from the French under Lafayette, finally prevailed against all the odds and defeated the hated Redcoats. The nation that would one day come to dominate the world was born. Now all was changed and those loyal to the Crown were forced to flee. Bryan's family was never in any real danger and his friendship with the new President ensured they did not suffer the fate of so many loyalist Tories. However, it certainly caused him to reflect upon his role in this brave new world. Bryan was approaching the age of fifty and once again began to reconsider his long-delayed plan to take Holy Orders. Before the Revolution, Virginia formed part of the Diocese of London but after Independence, the Church of England refused to recognise their former communicants in Virginia so there would be no ordinations or consecrations. However, the Episcopal Church of Scotland agreed to consecrate the American Samuel Seabury in Aberdeen in 1784. He returned to the United States and in 1789 Bryan was finally ordained by Bishop Seabury in Richmond. In the following year he was inducted as Rector of Fairfax Parish, at Christ Church, Alexandria and Falls Church. Both these 18th Century buildings survive today, little altered since Bryan's time. However, his tenure here was short lived and for some reason that no one has ever explained, he resigned as Rector in 1792 after only two years in his post - yet another change of direction in Bryan's complicated life.

Then in 1790, in yet another change of tack, Bryan sold Towlston Grange to George Washington for the princely sum of £82.10 and settled in a new home south of Hunting Creek, close to Alexandria, which he named Mount Eagle, in honour of his old friend and now President of the new nation.

When his cousin Robert, the 7th Lord Fairfax, died at Leeds Castle in 1793, Bryan had every right to assume the title. However, he clearly felt this was not appropriate and was content to style himself simply as 'the Reverend'. After all, he was now an American citizen and quite likely attached more importance to his position in the church than to an empty British title. He received nothing from his spendthrift cousin by way of inheritance and Leeds Castle itself went to his cousins the Martins, but when he travelled to England in 1798 he was surprised by the importance attached to his rank by everyone he met in London. We get an interesting sight of this curious colonial from a contemporary description:

> *'He was a large, handsome man of middle age, alert and vigorous, wearing a full suit of purple cloth with bands and powdered hair. His courteous manners, and his reputation for genuine piety and dignity of character won him many friends.'*

The purpose of Bryan's visit is unclear but luckily for us, a fascinating account of his time in England has come down to us in a letter he wrote home to his wife at Mount Eagle, dated 23rd September 1798. This long and rambling letter covers many matters, from his health, the people he met and the places he visited, what he ate and how much it cost, to more serious matters such as business meetings and his dealings with lawyers. These meetings are almost certainly the real reason for his visit, most likely with the agents upon whom he, like all planters in Virginia, still depended. As we have seen, their untrustworthiness and the financial distress they caused was one of the main reasons for the Revolution and little seems to have changed after Independence. When Bryan mentions his lack of money in the letter, as he frequently does, it was perhaps for this very reason.

The letter also tells us much about the character of this humble, God fearing man and his interest in those he meets. He begins with the observation that '*The people in this country live to a great age, two have died here in one week about 86…*' He visits his cousins at Leeds Castle, 'Dr Fairfax' (alias the Reverend Denny Martin who had taken the name Fairfax, as we saw earlier) and the latter's three sisters. Bryan noted, '*It was a pleasure to see a brother and three sisters living in harmony. I was quite in love with the sisters, indeed the brother I liked very much. He seems to be a worthy man.*' Surprisingly, he was less impressed with Leeds Castle itself, '*the whole rather inferior to Greenway Court.*' Quite a sweeping judgement of the 'loveliest castle in England' when one considers the reported simplicity of Lord Fairfax's remote Shenandoah homestead!

There is much talk of his poor health and state of mind, a life-long preoccupation – '*I have been much reduced and much more depressed than at any time for three years past*' – but is pleased to have found 'two surgeons and two apothecaries' to look after him.

Bryan was a man of strong religious convictions and had briefly served as the Rector of Christchurch, Alexandria, so it comes as no surprise that he writes extensively of *'an overruling Providence'* which guides and protects his every move: a bad storm when crossing the Atlantic abates thanks to Divine intercession and *'since I landed seen many instances of a kind Providence, in raising me up many friends, in having me placed both here and in London, in lodgings, where I meet with the civilest treatment – in falling into the hands of two eminent physicians, and when I wanted business in the law way, that I should be recommended first to Lord Buchan, and thro 'him to his brother,* (Thomas Erskine, afterwards Lord Chancellor) *who is one of the first Councillors in London….Have I not reason to be thankful and speak to the Glory of God, who befriends me in temporal as well as spiritual things.'*

His friend General Washington is also mentioned for his *'generosity who gave me letters of introduction, which have paved the way to these advantages. He gave me also a letter to Mr Strickland, who is as civil to me here, in York, as I could wish.'*

As for money we get these interesting observations, telling of his acute shortage of funds: *'I have yet, in a week or two, to go to London, chiefly upon business, and to return again in three weeks, in order to spend the Winter here. It will be expensive going and coming, but then it will be cheaper living here (in York). I am reduced to that pass, that I can't afford a servant and one horse…I had a hare for dinner today, given me by a friend, in the country. I am to have it hashed for supper. My landlady cooks my victuals for two shillings a week.'*

How bizarre it seems to us that a man with over 50,000 acres of Virginia could find himself in such a position.

Tantalizingly, he then goes on to talk of a *'Mrs Middleton of Kensington, perhaps I mentioned her before, as an old relation whom I knew before in London. She is now 76. She was very kind. I dined with her twice. She lives joining to the Palace, which has a door opening into the Park, as her house is one of the houses belonging to it.'*

One can only imagine just how amazed this Mrs Middleton and her distant cousin Bryan would have been to know that her descendant Katherine would also be living at Kensington Palace over two hundred years later, but now as the Duchess of Cambridge and our own future Queen!

It is not to the very end of this long, rambling letter that we get the briefest mention of his title: *'I have taken on me the title of Lord Fairfax which I should have done sooner, had I known it was becoming to do so.'*

Had he known the significance of this to later generations, he might have treated this matter with rather more seriousness. But that is the charm of this simple, pious, self-effacing man, and tells us so much more about his beliefs than anyone else could – that earthly titles are of little importance when compared to the Glory of God.

His meeting Lord Buchan and his brother Thomas Erskine, who Bryan claims as relations, certainly proved fortuitous. They took upon themselves to establish his right to the title of Lord Fairfax, and this was later confirmed on 6th May 1800. Bryan was the last member of the family to claim the title for over one hundred years. It would lie dormant until revived in 1908 by our grandfather whose task was made all the easier by Bryan's far-sighted decision.

Throughout his life Bryan had maintained the correspondence with his dear friend George Washington. The very last letter he received from his distinguished neighbour is dated 30th November 1799, less than a month before the President's death, in which he discusses boundaries between their mutual landholdings. Surprisingly for the head of the new Republic, he addresses his old friend as 'My Lord' in recognition of his new status. The week before the President's death, he and Martha dined with the Fairfax's at Mount Eagle and four days later on 11th December the hospitality was reciprocated when Bryan and his wife dined at Mount Vernon. The next day Washington rode out in freezing rain to inspect his farms, caught a chill and died on 14th December. In a letter to a cousin in England, Bryan quotes Dr James Craik, Washington's physician, as saying the First President's last words were: '*I die hard.*'

There was one final duty for Bryan to carry out and that was to act as one of the six official mourners at his old friend's funeral, which he did with his son Ferdinando, the President's godson. As a token of his respect, George left Bryan a large three-volume Bible which had belonged to the Bishop of Sodor and Man. In less than two years Bryan would join his friend when he died in 1802. A memorial stone stands to him at Ivy Hill Cemetery in Alexandria, where he lies surrounded by other members of the family.

Bryan had lived through turbulent times and although his life was characterised by a series of abrupt changes, he was consistent in his religious beliefs and a desire to seek peaceful compromise. He was also consistent in his friendship with his childhood friend and neighbour George Washington. Despite the different paths they took and the differing political views they held, they maintained a mutual respect and affection for one another that endured to the very end.

Part 2: Citizens of the Republic

10. The Bigger Picture

The page turns and the new century dawns. The world was changing and none more so than for the Fairfax family: from now on they saw themselves as American citizens through and through, with no concern for titles and barely a backwards glance at the old country. The death of Bryan Fairfax, coming soon after the start of the new century, drew a line in the sand for the family in Virginia; never again would they hold such positions of power and influence as they had in the 1700s nor stand so close to those in power. However, they did not slip entirely from view and over the course of the 19th century we will meet various remarkable members of the Fairfax family who would play their part in making America the great country it would become.

First, let us take a look at the bigger picture.

The central theme of American history in the first half of the 19th century is westward expansion. In later years this would be summed up in the phrase 'Manifest Destiny', a sentiment dreamed up in 1845 by the editor of New York Morning News, John O'Sullivan. It described a belief that Providence had given the United States a mission to spread Republican Democracy (and Protestant Christianity) throughout the whole of North America and hence the right to expand westwards, a sentiment with which few at the time would disagree.

When the thirteen states broke free from British rule they occupied a mere slice of the eastern seaboard that extended no further than the Appalachians; the rest of the continent that had been settled or claimed was in either Spanish, French or British hands. Vast stretches were still unclaimed, where only native Americans and the buffalo roamed. Over the course of the first half of the new century the United States would grow to occupy the whole of the continent south of the Canadian border and north of the Rio Grande - from 'Sea to Shining Sea'

The process would begin with the Louisiana Purchase of 1803: Napoleon Bonaparte, then First Consul of France, was short of funds to fight the British and their allies in Europe. He began negotiations to sell Louisiana to the United States. After much prevarication, Napoleon declared: 'Irresolution and deliberation are no longer in season. I renounce Louisiana.' And so the American negotiators James Monroe and Robert Livingstone persuaded their French counterparts to part with the whole of Louisiana, a vast territory which stretched from the Mississippi to the Rockies for the princely sum of $15 million. Amounting to 530 million acres, the Louisiana Purchase more than doubled the size of the existing USA as ceded by the British in 1783. At a mere 4 cents an acre, it must rate as the real estate bargain of all time!

Expansion continued with the acquisition of Florida from the Spanish in 1819. Then, in 1836 in what is today San Antonio, two hundred American settlers were surrounded and killed at a small mission called the Alamo. Revenge was swift and at the Battle of San Jacinto the Mexicans were defeated by the Texan army under Sam Houston to resounding cries of 'Remember the Alamo'. The President of Mexico, General Antonio Lopez de Santa Anna was among those captured and only released when he agreed to cede control of the whole of Texas. And so the Lone Star Republic was born.

Relations between Mexico and the United States remained fraught and finally came to a head when in 1845 Texas decided to join the Union. Then in 1846 and on the flimsiest of pretexts, President James A. Polk declared war on Mexico, a conflict that became known as the Mexican-

American War. When peace was finally declared in 1848 with the Treaty of Guadalupe Hildago, the Union would add both New Mexico and California to its territory, all for another $15 million. Large chunks of continents apparently came cheap in those days!

Quite by coincidence, in the very same year a certain Samuel Rogers, while building a lumber mill for one John Sutter in Coloma, California, noticed traces of gold in the mill race. With that, the California Gold Rush began. In no time at all the population of California would swell many fold as hopeful prospectors made the hazardous journey west to claim their share of the buried treasure.

And once again, as we will see, there would be Fairfax's in the thick of both these events.

As a footnote, Oregon, then still under British control also passed into American hands in 1846, after agreement to divide the territory along the 49th parallel. This completed the territorial expansion of the United States, with the exception of Alaska and Hawaii, which were both admitted into the Union in 1959 as the 49th and 50th States respectively.

11. Thomas the 9th Lord – Plain Mr Fairfax

Bryan's two surviving sons were Thomas and Ferdinando. As the elder, Thomas now had the right to style himself Lord Fairfax, but for him it held even less magic than it had for his father. This lack of interest in the trappings of the old order gives us a strong clue as to Thomas's character and attitudes. As we shall see, both these men embraced the new order willingly and looked to the future with a very different vision from their predecessors.

Thomas was born in 1762 probably at Green Hill or Belvoir, to Bryan's first wife Elizabeth Cary Fairfax. As we have seen his father was often absent and his mother in declining heath, so it fell to his remarkable sister Sally to bring him up until her untimely death at the age of 19. Thomas by contrast would go on to live to the considerable age of 84. He would marry three times: Mary Aylett being his first wife, Louisa Washington his second and Margaret Herbert his third.

The latter two were his cousins: Louisa was the daughter of Warner Washington, son of the President's cousin John Washington and his wife Hannah, a daughter of Colonel William Fairfax and Thomas's grandfather.

Margaret was the granddaughter of Major John Carlyle and his wife Sarah Fairfax, another daughter of Colonel William Fairfax. Margaret, whom he married in 1800, would bear all his ten children.

Thomas was given a tract of land at Towlston by his father in a deed dated 1st October 1788 and here he set about building his first home known as Ash Grove. The house is located close to Tyson's Corner at the intersection of Leesburg Pike and Dulles Access Road and happily still stands today. This house occupied the site of a hunting lodge built by the 6th Lord Fairfax, known as the 'White

House', which was moved to make way for the new construction.

Thomas lived at Ash Grove for many years and passed it to his second son Henry on his marriage in 1827. Then Thomas moved to another house known as Vaucluse, not far away on the heights above Alexandria. This had previously belonged to Dr James Craik, George Washington's personal physician, and here the family would live until 1861 when it was occupied by the Union Army and pulled down to make way for the military defence of Washington. As we shall see, Vaucluse would come to occupy an almost mystical place in the psyche of later members of the family, symbolising with its cruel destruction every loss the family had to endure during the Civil War.

When his father died in 1802, Thomas was by then aged 40 and quite old enough to know his own mind. His chief activity was farming, the staple crop being the tobacco with which the name of Virginia is inextricably linked.

In some respects, his life was somewhat similar to his father's, which apart from administering his extensive plantations of some 40,000 acres, involved hunting and attending social functions. Like his father he too held strong religious convictions He never went as far as taking holy orders, being altogether more unconventional. Eschewing his father's adherence to the Episcopalian Church, Thomas became a follower of the 18th century Christian mystic visionary Emmanuel Swedenborg.

Swedenborg's belief was that the established church would be replaced by a 'New Church' that worshipped God in the form of one person alone, Jesus Christ. It also espoused a more humane belief that all men are created equal irrespective of their creed or colour. This was part of the 'Second Great Awakening', the great Christian religious revival movement that emerged at the beginning of the 19th

century and is seen as the starting point of the movement for the abolition of slavery.

The process of freeing slaves, 'manumission', was enthusiastically adopted in the Upper South, particularly in Delaware, Maryland and Northern Virginia after 1776. Many thousands of slaves were freed, and the population of freed slaves rose from one to ten per cent in the two decades following this date. By 1810 three-quarters of all slaves in Delaware were free. Among the most notable individuals to embrace this were Robert Carter III, a descendant of 'King' Carter, the 6th Lord's original agent in the Northern Neck Proprietary. In 1791 he freed more than 450 people by a 'Deed of Gift', the largest number any single American would ever free. By 1860, 91.7 per cent of blacks were free in Delaware and 49.7 per cent in Maryland.

This movement certainly appealed to Thomas's humane nature and religious beliefs and over the course of his life he would free more than one hundred slaves. He would teach them a trade and then re-employ them, or send them to Pennsylvania. Some were encouraged to settle in Liberia, a new state established on the west coast of Africa for freed slaves. However it was frequently the case that the freed slaves proved incapable of caring for themselves and these Thomas continued to support throughout their lives.

As we have already seen, Thomas was a man with an enquiring mind and open to new ideas, as his unorthodox religious beliefs and decision to free his slaves demonstrate. He was also a practical fellow and has been described as an inventor and craftsman. Although we have no record of any significant inventions of his, he had his own forge and workshop, where he fashioned a pair of lightning rods that were installed on the roof of Ash Grove. Of course it was famously Benjamin Franklin who in 1749 invented the lightning rod, but Thomas Fairfax's adoption of this new technology is almost certainly the reason Ash Grove survived so long.

Thomas's interest in science and progress is of no consequence in the much larger story of the Industrial Revolution, but it does show us that he was keenly aware of new ideas and developments that were taking place around him.

Taken together these three aspects of Thomas's life, his non-conformist religious beliefs, his humanity, especially in his attitude to slavery and his interest in science and technology, mark him out as a very different individual from his forebears and in these respects he was a 'moderniser' who eagerly embraced new ideas and attitudes.

12. The Journey

In 1936, my grandfather Albert, the 12th Lord Fairfax, came upon a small hand-made octavo volume among his papers. This turned out to be the record of a journey Thomas the 9th Lord had made from Virginia to Salem, Massachusetts in 1799 and is one of the most illuminating records we have of Thomas and the times in which he lived. Albert published it in an elegant edition with line drawings of 250 copies 'for private circulation', one of which is in front of me as I write.

The original manuscript was written in Thomas's own hand on 44 leaves of thin Eagle watermark paper and is an intimate record of his observations and thoughts along the arduous journey. As with all diaries it also tells us much more about the author himself - his attitudes, interests and prejudices – than any second hand description could. It shows us that Thomas was a man with an enquiring mind who paints a vivid picture of American life in this early stage of its development.

The purpose of the journey was ostensibly to visit relations of his grandmother Deborah Clarke, second wife of Colonel William Fairfax, who was born in Salem. However when he actually arrives, there is barely a mention of his relations apart from a brief note that he 'received from them many civilities'. After two days he set off again on his way home. At the end of his story he tells us that 'The writing of it has served to fill up some intervals of time which might otherwise have passed more heavily…'

Time might well have passed quite heavily, as not only was travelling a slow business in those days, but there was also much Thomas wanted to forget: As we know in the previous four years he had lost two wives in quick succession, his first wife Mary Aylett died six months after their marriage in November 1795 and then his second wife and cousin

The Journey

Louisa Washington, whom he had married in February 1798, died two months later. Perhaps he felt a long journey would help heal the sadness of these losses. Whatever the case Thomas had more luck with his third wife, also a cousin. She was Margaret Herbert, whom he married shortly after his return in 1800; she went on to bear him ten children and would outlive him by twelve years, surviving until 1858.

The real pleasure of Thomas's journal lies in his descriptions of the places and people he meets along the way. It also gives us some idea of the sheer effort required to travel any distance in those days before the steam train or paddle steamer.

The story begins as he sets off from home to find a ship: '*On the first day of August 1799 I left Fairfield in Frederick County in the family Carriage, and passing the River Shannandoah at Wormley's Ferry, pursued the road over the mountain towards Leesburg. In descending the mountain, the eye is presented with a most engaging landscape formed by the lowlands stretching to the north east to an extent of several miles, and diversified with alternate fields and woodlands...*'

His plan was to take ship in Alexandria for Boston but finding none available he decides to go on to Norfolk. The rate of progress by our standards was impossibly slow and involved overnight stops at Fredericksburg, Richmond, Petersburg, Smithfield and finally Norfolk. However, this slow pace gives us some interesting and amusing snippets of life in those far-off times:

In Richmond he was '*entertained with an agreeable serenade, by a black man who had taken his stand near the Tavern, and for the amusement of those of his colour, sung and played on the Bangoe. He appeared to be quite an adept on the African instrument, which tho' it may not bear comparison with the guitar, is certainly capable of conveying much pleasure to a musical ear. Its wild notes of melody seem to correspond with the state of civilization of the country where this species of music originated.*' So it seems Thomas was an early jazz fan.

Shortly afterwards Thomas had a hair-raising ride experience involving a carriage driver who had '*a drink too much*' and drove his horses at '*an unmerciful rate*', egged on by a group of equally inebriated seafarers and 'commercial men'. It was not until the driver had fallen asleep that they came to their senses and managed to bring the careering vehicle to a halt. The shaken Thomas notes that travellers should on no account treat their driver to liquor before his day's work is done.

When Thomas finally arrives in Norfolk two weeks after leaving home he finds a small brig bound for New York and so they set sail. With a fair wind this passage should have taken only three days but due to head winds it was ten days before New York came into sight. However, the journey was not over yet, as yellow fever was rife in the city and their ship was put into quarantine, obliging the captain to ride out at anchor until cleared by a physician. New York, then as now, was a beautiful city but Thomas's remarks as they approach are double edged: '*Nothing can be more beautiful than the approach to the City by this channel, yet I could not help comparing it to the painted Sepulchre; beautiful without, but full of death, and infection within.*' So without delay he finds another ship bound for Rhode Island and is on his way within two hours.

This time the wind is fair and the ship covers the two hundred miles from New York to Newport Rhode Island in less than two days. Here again they were forced to 'ride quarantine' until approval was given for them to land. After some approving remarks as to Newport's general appearance he sets off in the stage coach for Providence.

Yellow fever was an ever-present danger and frequently fatal. In 1793 there was a major outbreak in Philadelphia, the seat of George Washington's government, which led to several thousand deaths and the speedy departure of the administration to Trenton where it was still sitting in 1799.

Overall, it is estimated that as many as 150,000 people died of yellow fever in the USA during the 18th and 19th centuries. It was not until 1927 that the yellow fever virus was isolated in West Africa leading to the development of two vaccines in the 1930s and its eradication in large parts of the world.

Throughout Thomas's account there are continual comments on the countryside, the state of the roads, his lodgings and the quality of the food. His more interesting comments are reserved for his fellow travellers; some he clearly prefers to others, such as the two young ladies he sits with from Providence to Boston, *'whose singing and lively chat contributed much to our amusement.'* Others he finds much less attractive, such as one group, some of whom were so 'corpulent' that he is forced to ride outside with the driver!

Finally he arrives in Salem on 31st August, almost exactly a month after leaving his home in Virginia.

Two days later he is on his way home again, but this time he chooses the overland route. His first stop is Boston where he is wildly impressed by all he sees: the bridge over the Charles River, nearly a mile in length, gets a mention, but it is the recently completed State House with its huge dome, fifty feet across and forty feet high that really attracts his attention. Ever the scientist, he makes careful notes of its construction pointing out that many of the slates on its roof have already slipped off leaving the shingles underneath bare. He is also very struck by the fact that anyone can walk in and look at the many books and papers in the various offices *'so that people so disposed might commit thefts and depredations without detection.'*

The next stop is Providence, where he visits Brown University, noting that it has fifty-six rooms, a library of two thousand volumes and *'Philosophical Apparatus'* (instruments for experiments). Providence is clearly a prosperous place, with many fine buildings and churches, which he tells us is the result of its trade with both the West and East Indies, exceeding those of Alexandria or Newport.

Of course by the standards of our secular age, we would find people in those times hilariously priggish and the next episode illustrates just that: Thomas arrives in the town of Norwich, Connecticut, on a Sunday, and naturally goes to church. Sitting close by he spots a young lady, *'who with the soft lustre of her eyes, seemed calculated to draw off the attention of all the young men, in the vicinity of her pew, from the service of the day.'* Well, what did he expect? Thomas is horrified and goes on to propose a remarkably stern, but to us hilarious solution to the problem of pretty young ladies distracting young men from their higher thoughts in church.

Thomas's proposal is this: a committee consisting of '*three men of taste*' entitled '*Ye Committee of Beauty*' should meet every six months with the solemn purpose of closely inspecting the face of each girl aged fourteen or thereabouts. Notes would be taken and after dismissing the girls, 'Ye Committee' would decide which girls might be a cause for distraction among the young men folk in the congregation. Those deemed too pretty for the public good would '*be forbidden, under a certain penalty, from appearing thereafter at Church unless with a double veil of gause.*' One can just imagine the clamour to join 'Ye Committee.'

There is no record if anything ever came of Thomas's stern proposals, but as my grandfather Albert points out in his notes to the book, it was a quaint idea that a Cavalier from Virginia might want to add anything to the Puritan 'blue laws' of Connecticut!

And so the slow journey continues. In Newhaven he sees the 'The Neptune', a large ship recently returned from a long and fruitful voyage to the South Seas and India, '*by which I was told immense returns were made to her owners.*' He passes by a '*remarkable place called Horseneck*' the scene of a daring escape from the British by the legendary hero of the

Revolutionary War, General Israel Putnam down a sheer cliff. He adds that on another occasion this same brave man had the *'temerity to crawl upon hands and knees into a low cave to attack a wolf !'* He obviously admires the General and when taken with other disparaging remarks about the 'British', there is no question as to where his loyalties lie.

Arriving in New York State, where he puts up at an attractive house in sight of Long Island which is *'what every townsman are daily sighing for, that is, a snug little retreat in the country'*. But the lady of the house is unhappy with her lot and leads Thomas to conclude that happiness is not a place, but in the mind. A statement that is as true today as it was then.

The diary is full of interesting observations. Around New York, Thomas notes that an acre sells for as much as £100, a huge amount at the time. In New Jersey he meets a farmer who has been offered £20 per acre for his farm, which he adds is equivalent to £15 'Virginia currency' and is the reason so many farmers were selling up and moving to the south where a man from the northern states with 100 acres could buy 300.

In Trenton, which he notes is the home to many *'different Officers of Government'*, who had fled from the yellow fever epidemic in Philadelphia, he is entertained by a *'Mr Cook, celebrated for the powers of his voice'*, accompanied by a pleasant new form of musical instrument consisting of a series of bells suspended in a row from a beam. Similar cow bell instruments are still found today in Switzerland and Germany, and as many Germans had settled there, this is likely to be their origin.

In Pennsylvania he crosses the Susquehannah River, where he tells us with amusement that the ferry-house keepers on either side are a Mr Stump and a Mr Stake. Mr Stump, of German extraction, provides an excellent table for the weary traveller consisting of *'two sorts of fish, fresh vegetables, some excellent tarts and cheese, and half a pint of wine, the whole for 2/6 Virginia currency.'* No mention is made of Mr Stake's offerings.

Finally he arrives at Harper's Ferry and here his poor horse is injured disembarking from the ferry, leaving a large gash in his thigh. Luckily the horse makes a full recovery and by nightfall he is at Shannon Hill, the home of his brother Ferdinando.

In the final paragraph of the diary he concludes that while this account of his journey, *'however barren of incident it may appear, and how little interesting to the few who will ever peruse it, will yet be considered, that useful information is not to be acquired by an hasty progression through a country, where the only mediums of knowledge one has access to are uninformed innkeepers and travellers.'*

With that the journal ends. Although one must agree that nothing very dramatic happens on his journey, he is wrong to assume it will not be of interest to later readers, such as ourselves some two hundred years later. A diary is such a wonderful thing: not only does it show us the world first hand as the author saw it, it also tells us so much more about the author than any third party might. Descriptions of the everyday, however mundane and commonplace they may seem to the author, are of course fascinating to later generations and teach us so much more than the big events of history ever do.

13. Ferdinando Fairfax 1766 – 1820

Before we hear about Thomas and Margaret Fairfax's children, I must first tell you the sad story of his unfortunate brother Ferdinando.

Like his elder brother, Ferdinando was a kind, compassionate and deeply religious man. Like his brother he too inherited substantial estates and could have spent his life quietly enjoying their benefits. But sadly Ferdinando made the fatal mistake of embarking on various wild business schemes that would lead to the loss of his entire fortune by the time of his death. Ferdinando was born with every advantage in life, topped off by having the future First President as his godfather. Together with his father he would later play the role of official mourner at his godfather's funeral, a singular honour indeed. Of more immediate value however was the immense inheritance he received from his uncle George William Fairfax upon his deathin England in 1787. The childless George William had made the young Ferdinando his heir and so around the time of his 21st birthday not only did he became the owner of the disputed estates in Yorkshire but also immense tracts of Virginia. There was Belvoir on the Potomac, land in the Piedmont and the 29,000 acre Shannondale tract near Harpers Ferry in what is today West Virginia.

He married a cousin Elizabeth Blair Cary of Ceely's in 1796 and the young couple lived for a while on the Belvoir plantation, although not of course in the fine mansion his grandfather had built. That had burned down and now lay in mournful ruin. Instead they lived at the more modest 'White House', below the cliffs near the shoreline of the Potomac. Here he gained a reputation for good works, giving large sums to worthy causes such as free schools and public libraries. Like his brother Thomas, Ferdinando was a follower of Emmanuel Swedenborg. Accordingly he found slavery abhorrent and over the course of his life he freed many of his slaves, settling them with family members on the stipulation that they must never be sold on. In 1790 he published his *Plan for Liberating the Negroes within the United States*, in which he advocated the gradual abolition of slavery by way of manumission. The government would compensate slave owners for the loss of their 'property' and the former slaves would be settled to live separately from white society.

So, Ferdinando was a true pillar of the community and greatly respected by all. He was also a man of action and during the War of 1812 against the British played an important role in the defence of Washington, being commended for his bravery there. It was during this campaign that theremaining structure of the Belvoir mansion was finally destroyed to make way for a gun battery to bombard the British fleet as it sailed away down the Potomac.

With a fast growing family that would eventually number sixteen children,the busy couple decided to move out to the remote Shannondale tract, where they settled not far from Harpers Ferry, just across the Shennandoah River from what would become Shannondale Springs. They called their home Shannon Hill and doubtless felt life was full of promise. Instead, this is where it all began to go wrong for the luckless Ferdinando.

In a nut shell the sad story is this: encouraged by the neighbouring landowners John Semple and Henry Lee, Fairfax decided to exploit the rich iron ore resources that lay under his property. He also set about timber felling and planted the land to raise crops. In the process he borrowed huge sums to finance these enterprises but found himself unable to sell his products. There is no known explanation for this sad state of affairs, although my theory is that his stance on slavery had infuriated the slave owning and trading lobby to such an extent that they conspired in his downfall. Whatever the reason, in the end, weighed down with debt and law suits, he was forced to sell off most of his vast inheritance to repay hiscreditors. When he died at the relatively early age of 54, the WashingtonGazette recorded his passing in this way:

> *'The Hon. Ferdinando Fairfax died in the 26th, transferred from being a member of the New Church, at Mount Eagle near Alexandria, to be one of the same church in Heaven. Descendant of Sir Thomas Fairfax who commanded the Republican vs. Royal army at Marsden Moor (sic). Godson of George Washington and inherited many of his milder virtues. He was a polite and accomplished gentleman, possessed of every kind of knowledge except worldly - he was sober, frugal and industrious, yet more money escaped from him than from any other man. He has left an unsullied character to enlighten the paths of honour and virtue to a numerous and hopeful progeny.'*

And so ends the sad tale of Ferdinando. Even if he left his children no pecuniary legacy, he at least left them with something of the old Fairfax fighting spirit. From among his many offspring, his eldest son George William, by his marriage to Isabella, (daughter of Major W. Gibbs McNeill of New York) produced a very remarkable son, Donald McNeill Fairfax. As we shall see in a later chapter, Donald would rise to the rank of Rear-Admiral and was the only member of the Fairfax family to side with the Union in the Civil War, playing a key role in one of its most pivotal moments. Once again there would be a Fairfax present at a crucial moment in history.

14. The Children of Thomas and Margaret Fairfax

Thomas and Margaret's marriage was a happy one and soon there were ten children to feed, clothe and educate. Sad to say, three of their children, Raymond, Ethelbert and Lavinia, were not destined to live beyond childhood. Although this is shocking to us, this was not considered unusual in those times as infant mortality rates were high. Even so, one can only imagine how distressing it must have been for the parents.

Their eldest son was Albert and although he would die young, before his father, he had time to marry and produce two sons, both of whom would be entitled to call themselves Lord Fairfax. Their second son, Henry, a great patriot, would win fame for raising his own company to fight in the Mexican-American War before he succumbed to yellow fever. Orlando, their third son, would become a well-respected doctor in Alexandria while Reginald, a Lieutenant in the US Navy, sided with the Confederacy during the Civil War. He too died before his time, aged forty, in 1862. Their three other daughters, Eugenia, Aurelia and Monimia were luckier and all lived to marry, have children and reach a reasonable age.

So let us now meet the next generation of the Fairfax family, the children of Thomas 9th Lord Fairfax and his wife Margaret.

Albert and the Snowden Family

It is said that their eldest son Albert (1802-35) was blessed with outstanding good looks and this may have had something to do with his capturing the heart of the daughter of one of Maryland's most prominent families, the Snowdens of Prince George's County. The young lady was Caroline Eliza Snowden, the daughter of Richard Snowden and his wife Eliza Warfield of Longwood in Howard County, another well to do Maryland family. A later member of the Warfield family would one day rise to fame, or notoriety, as the woman who stole the heart, but not the crown, of a British monarch - Wallis Simpson was of course born a Warfield - and following the abdication of King Edward VIII, she became his wife and Duchess of Windsor.

The Snowdens originally came from Wales, but later moved to Birmingham, England. Richard Snowden (the elder) was born in 1640 at a tumultuous time in British history: the English Civil War was on the verge of breaking out and this would in turn lead to the King's defeat and eventual execution in 1649.

Richard's family were supporters of Oliver Cromwell's Parliamentarians, who would cast their dour shadow over the country for the next nine years. When Cromwell unexpectedly died in 1658, the young Richard sensed trouble ahead and so in the same year set sail for Maryland, an area sympathetic to Republican Puritans.

This turned out to be a wise decision, for many supporters of Cromwell's regime did indeed meet a grisly end. More to the point, it marked the beginning of a rapid climb in the fortunes of the Snowden family that in three generations would see them established as among the richest and most powerful in Colonial America.

The family prospered and his grandson Richard, known as 'the Ironmaster', established the Patuxent Iron Work Company in 1736; other enterprises would follow, such as a grist mill and biscuit factory on the Hawling River. Over the course of his lifetime he amassed a great fortune and by the time of his death in 1763 his estate included Snowden Hall, Fairland, Montpelier, Oakland, Snow Hill, Avondale, Woodland Hill, Alnick, Elmwood, Brightwood, Maple Grove, and most of the land that comprises modern-day Laurel in Maryland. In other words, he was the archetypical

American tycoon, long before America actually came into being. It will also be no surprise to learn that the Snowdens were Quakers, as were so many of the architects of America's economic power.

Future generations of the Snowden family would build on the Ironmaster's success and several fine mansions remain as testament to their wealth and power. Among these are Montpelier, Oaklands, Snow Hill and Engleside. Even in Maryland today, to say you are related to the Snowdens can attract considerable prestige.

Caroline Eliza Snowden's grandfather, Major Thomas Snowden (himself the grandson of Richard, the Ironmaster), was a celebrated hero of the Revolutionary War and served under George Washington. With his wife Anne Dorsey Ridgely, he lived at Montpelier, a beautiful Georgian mansion in Laurel, where they entertained their many guests lavishly, among them George Washington in 1787. This striking house is now a National Historic Landmark and open to the public.

Major Thomas gave another beautiful house, Oaklands, to his son Richard and it was here that Caroline Eliza was born and raised.

Although his life was to be short, Albert and his wife Caroline Eliza produced two sons and thus continued the line of the Fairfax peerage, ignored and largely forgotten though it was. Their eldest son Charles eagerly joined the Gold Rush to California and would leave behind a town named after him. His second son John became a doctor and succeeded his brother as the nominal 11th Lord Fairfax. It was his eldest son, another Albert, who would go on to re-establish the Fairfax family once again in England and take his rightful place in the House of Lords.

Henry Fairfax, 'Hero' of the Mexican-American War

Thomas and Margaret Fairfax's second son Henry was born in 1804 and always dreamed of pursuing a military career. Quite likely he had been weaned on tales of his famous ancestor Sir Thomas 'Black Tom' Fairfax's exploits in the English Civil War. His wish would eventually come true but not with the glorious outcome he might have hoped for. After a false start at Columbia College (now George Washington University) Henry enrolled at the United States Military College. Unfortunately, ill health thwarted his ambitions and reluctantly he returned home, marrying his cousin Ann Caroline Herbert in 1827. Henry and his bride set up home at the family seat Ash Grove, where they raised six children, of whom the three eldest boys would go on to serve in the Confederate Army.

Henry's parents meanwhile moved to Vaucluse near Alexandria, which would remain the principal Fairfax home until 1861 when Union forces raised the house to the ground at the start of the Civil War.

So for the next twenty years, Henry led the happy life of a gentleman farmer, and a successful one too, for in 1847 he was made President of the Lewinsville Farmers' Association. He gave generously to the restoration of Falls Church and in 1840 and 1841 was a lay delegate to the Diocesan Convention. However, his interest in all things military was never far from his mind and despite his early failure to gain a commission in the regular army, he served for a number of years as captain of a reserve cavalry company attached to the 6th (Fairfax County) Regiment of the Virginia Militia.

Life might have carried on in this quiet way for Henry but then in 1846, two things happened that would change his life: firstly, his father, the aged Thomas, the 9th Lord, finally died. Whether this spurred him to action we cannot say, but he now had less reason to feel duty bound to stay at home;

secondly, in an act of pure adventurism, the United States declared war on Mexico.

The last time the United States had been at war was against the British in 1812 and few had any recollection of just what war entailed. As we know only too well, there is nothing glorious or heroic about war, but to Henry's generation it held a promise of excitement and glory. At least that was Henry's view and here at last was an opportunity to rally to the colours and fight bravely for his country as he always dreamed he would. But how would he do this? After all, he was well over forty by now and quite past the age for active service. Henry was not to be thwarted, and, swept up by a tide of patriotic fervour, he decided to raise his own company of volunteers. After much delay and a direct appeal to President Polk himself, he finally managed to enrol some forty volunteers into Fairfax's Company at Fairfax Court House on 1st March 1847. Subsequently mustered into the United States Army at Fort Washington in Maryland, they began their long journey towards south to confront the enemy, or so they thought. Henry was nothing if not a patriot but his dreams of military glory would end in disaster.

Travelling by steamboat down the Ohio and Mississippi Rivers, they eventually arrived in New Orleans, from where they took ship to Port Isabel in Mexico arriving in late April. If the volunteers imagined they would be thrust straight into battle they were to be sorely disappointed. Most of May was spent in long and arduous marches into the baking interior of Mexico until they eventually arrived at Camp Buena Vista near Saltillo. By now they were thoroughly worn out and disgruntled. Still there was no prospect of the glorious action Henry and his men had hoped for. Nor would there be, for they remained at the camp throughout the summer, learning the rudiments of drill and the hard life of a soldier.

Life for the recruits was tough and punishments were exceedingly cruel by our standards. These included standing on the head of a barrel for two hours a day, for two weeks, and hard labour with ball and chain. For more serious offences, a man could be forced to stand in the sun all day, with his outstretched arms tied to a musket, which was in turn tied to a pole. This was not at all as Henry had imagined soldiering would be and doubtless he was disillusioned, although he kept his thoughts to himself. To his men he was always a 'can-do' cheerleader. Light relief came on the 4th of July when the hard regime was suspended for a day of celebration culminating in a fine dinner attended by their Divisional Commander General John Ellis Wool, something which did much to restore morale among Fairfax's men.

However, the high morale did not last as tragedy was soon to follow. Brave Henry, so eager to taste battle, was struck down not by the enemy but by a fever and died early in August, having never fired a shot in anger. Although his death was not the glorious one he might have hoped for, it brought a degree of fame and praise he never received whilst alive. An officer wrote of him: 'He was a most excellent man and a good officer and we shall feel his loss sensibly.' Orders were later published paying tribute to a faithful officer who, 'If opportunity in the field had offered, would have done signal honour to his eminent ancestry, to the service and to his country.' Henry's body was temporarily interred at Monterrey until arrangements could be made to ship it home. When word reached Virginia of his death, the Gazette eulogised that the officers and men were warmly attached to their captain and that, 'They regarded him as a friend and a brother as well as respected him as a commander.' The Fairfax County Court, of which he had been a member, adopted resolutions and agreed to wear a badge of mourning for thirty days.

When peace was eventually declared in 1848, Henry's remains were disinterred and shipped home, arriving in Alexandria on 1st August aboard the steamboat Osceola. Ships in the harbour flew their flags at half-mast and the Alexandria Artillery fired minute guns in respect. A long line of uniformed militiamen, their arms reversed and flags shrouded, escorted the hearse to the armoury for the funeral rites. To crown the ceremonial, George Washington Parke Custis, a step-grandson of George Washington, delivered the principal address.

Henry was finally laid to rest at Falls Church where his memorial stone can be seen today, with this inscription: 'In memory of Henry Fairfax, an accomplished gentleman, an upright magistrate, a sincere Christian, died in command of the Fairfax Volunteers, at Saltillo, Mexico, 1847. But for his munificence, this church might still have been a ruin.'

What Henry's wife and children felt about Henry's posthumous heroic status we can only guess. One imagines they might have preferred a living husband and father to a dead hero but history does not relate. However, we do know that in 1851, his widow Ann was obliged to sell Ash Grove to William Sherman which would indicate a change in the family's fortunes. So ended the Fairfax's long-standing connection with that historic property.

Dr Orlando Fairfax, a Southern Loyalist

Thomas and Margaret's third son, Orlando (1806-82), was a respected doctor who lived with his wife (and cousin) Mary Randolph Cary in a beautiful house that had been built by his father on Cameron Street, Alexandria. This historic house still stands today. Unfortunately, he was ruined by his decision to invest in Confederate bonds and his latter days were spent in greatly reduced circumstances. Three of their sons served in the Confederate Army and one of them, Randolph, was killed at the Battle of Fredericksburgh in

1862. In 1866 their daughter Monimia married George Davies, former Attorney-General of the Confederate States.

Reginald Fairfax, the Naval Officer

Their next son, Reginald (1822-62), was a career naval officer, but when the Civil War broke out, like most Virginians he rallied to the Confederate flag, holding the rank of Commander in the Confederate Navy. He died in 1862, a victim of malaria, but despite his allegiance to the rebel cause, he had shrewdly invested the fortune he received from his father in Federal bonds, to the great benefit of his sisters who were his heirs.

Eugenia, Aurelia and Monimia Fairfax

Of Thomas and Margaret's surviving daughters, Eugenia (1814-1880) married twice, first Edgar Mason of Gunston Hall fame and a grandson of George Mason, and second Charles Hyde, and between them she had six children. Aurelia (1816-1884) married Colonel James Irwin of Kentucky and had two children. The last child, Monimia (1820–1875), married another cousin, Archibald Cary of Cumberland, Maryland. Of her three children, Constance is best remembered as a writer: a strong supporter of the Confederate cause and keeper of the Fairfax flame, Constance firmly nailed her colours to the mast when in 1866 she married Colonel Burton Harrison, Secretary to Jefferson Davis, President of the Confederate States throughout the war.

So as you can see, to say the Fairfax's were true Sons and Daughters of Dixie would be something of an understatement.

Part 3: The Golden West

15. Charles Snowden Fairfax – The Californian Baron

In 2002, my wife Victoria and I decided to take our three children to visit her uncle in California. Uncle Richard, the brother of my wife's late Danish mother, had emigrated to San Francisco in the 1950s and was now living in retirement in Northern California not far from Sausalito in Marin County. Eagerly we planned our trip and carefully studied the maps. The idea was to spend a few days in Northern California before heading south down the Big Sur towards Los Angeles. It was then we spotted it, right there before our eyes and not a stone's throw from where Uncle Richard lived: the town of Fairfax.

I began to recall a visitor some twenty years before who had come to our family home near Maidenhead in search of the present-day Fairfax family, after whose ancestor her little town in Northern California was named. Our visitor, Patricia Arrigoni, was studying in London at the time and had made it her business to track us down. Now it all came back to me and with it, her stories of how 'Charlie' Fairfax had made the hazardous journey west in 1850, lured on by tales of the fortune to be made in the gold fields. To say we were amazed by this information is an understatement; here was a whole new dimension to the saga of our American forebears that been entirely forgotten. Without Patricia's initiative, things might not have turned out as they did and we will always be grateful to her for opening the door to us.

I have to admit that in those intervening years I had not given much thought to our Californian ancestor or the town named after him, although its presence never entirely escaped me. Rather like Sleeping Beauty, the memory just needed re-awakening. With our trip to California imminent, that moment had arrived and I reached for the telephone…

The warmth of our welcome in Fairfax is something we will never forget. There were parades, speeches and proclamations. A grand lunch was held in our honour and presentations were made: a Stars and Stripes flag that had been flown over the Capitol in Washington DC on the Fourth of July, a California Bear Flag flown over the State Capitol in Sacramento and to cap it all, a ceremonial key to the Town of Fairfax! Truly we were overwhelmed. The local press trumpeted our arrival and we have never felt more like royalty, nor are we likely to again. After an absence of one hundred and thirty-four years, the Fairfax's had come home to California!

However, it occurred to me that the person the residents of Fairfax, California were really honouring that day was not me nor my family but my great-grand-uncle, Charles Snowden, 10th Lord Fairfax.

So what was it that made Charlie, as he was always known, such a popular figure, that his memory should be so cherished after so long and a town named in his honour?

Let us now join Charlie Fairfax and hear of his remarkable life in the Golden West.

Charles Snowden Fairfax was the eldest son of the handsome Albert Fairfax and his wife Caroline Eliza Snowden. Born in 1829, he and his younger brother John, born a year later, were raised at his grandparents' house Vaucluse, high above Alexandria. Here they grew up surrounded by their many cousins.

One can imagine the happy but chaotic domestic scene at Vaucluse in those early years; perhaps it was this that gave Charlie his love of good company and a party, something for which he would become so well-known later in California.

However, a dark shadow was soon to intrude upon this happy scene and when Charlie was six, his father Albert died aged just thirty-three. This was a great blow but, as families do, they rallied to the occasion and soon his mother remarried a career army officer, William Sanders. She would live to the grand old age of 91, dying in the last year of the century. What amazing changes she would see in her long life!

Charlie's childhood was by all accounts a happy one and under the benign influence of his grandfather, Thomas 9th Lord Fairfax, he absorbed his liberal attitudes, treating both slave and free man alike. As we know, Thomas was an early abolitionist, employing many former slaves to work as paid employees. So in this congenial atmosphere Charlie grew to be a man and friend to all. He learnt all the usual skills of a country boy such as hunting and fishing and was said to be adept with a gun. Later he was sent to Cincinnati, Ohio to study law. It is quite possible that here he met the woman who would later become his wife, Ada Benham, the daughter of a well-known Cincinnati family.

Knowing what we do of Charlie now, it is hard to imagine him settling down to the somewhat humdrum life of a lawyer in Cincinnati; but luckily for him events were about to take a turn that would propel him on a far more adventurous course than he could have possibly ever imagined. For this was 1849 and the California Gold Rush had begun. The cry rang out '*Go West, Young Man!*' and so they did in their tens of thousands, among them the young Charles Snowden Fairfax.

Charlie was by now twenty years old and by rights head of the Fairfax family, as the 10th Lord. However, the life of a gentleman plantation owner held little appeal for this charming and energetic young man. His grandfather had finally died in 1846 at the grand old age of 84 and his mother now lived in Washington DC. Two of his aunts, Eugenia and Monimia, had also married, leaving only Aurelia to care for his grandmother Margaret, who would live on until 1858. His younger brother John had enrolled at the University of Pennsylvania where he would matriculate in medicine. So there was little to keep him at home and in any case with the whole world California-bound, how could he possibly resist the prospect of an adventure and the riches it promised?

Charlie joined a band known as the Virginia Company, among whose members was his mother's cousin, Richard Snowden. Uncle Dick, as he was known, seems to have been a fairly unattractive character: he had gambled away two family houses in Maryland and was now running away from his wife. California seemed the ideal refuge for him, where the lure of an easy fortune in the gold fields was his best hope. Later they would be joined by his two sons, Richard Nicholas Snowden and Gustavus Warfield Snowden, but only tragedy awaited them. All three would meet violent ends in California.

They found a ship suitable for their adventure, the Glenmore, which they filled with the finest Virginia tobacco, mining equipment and other supplies, which they hoped to sell to other prospectors when they arrived in California. Setting off on 2nd April 1849, the ship finally arrived seven months later on 6th October. However, Charlie was not on the Glenmore when it arrived, as has generally been thought, but actually arrived eight months later in the summer of 1850 on another ship, the California. We know this from one of the passengers of the Glenmore, Dr J.W. Claiborne, whose 1890 book *The Argonauts of California* gave the passenger manifest and there was no mention of a Charles Fairfax. (It seems likely that he left the Glenmore at

Panama and joined the California on the Pacific Coast.) One passenger who was on the Glenmore, however, was Alfred Taliaferro, a good friend of Charlie's and someone who would later on play an important role in his life.

Looking back over the 150 years since the Gold Rush began, it is easy for us to underestimate the enormous challenges this epic journey presented. There was no transcontinental railroad, that would only come some twenty years later, and the option of a wagon train across the plains and then the Rockies was not something anyone would relish. The only realistic alternative was to go by sea and this is how anyone who could afford it travelled to the West Coast. Even then it was a daunting prospect. The choice was either a voyage of several months around Cape Horn, as in the case of the Glenmore, or the shorter (but by no means less hazardous) alternative of taking a ship to the east coast of Panama, then going by foot or mule train across the disease-ridden isthmus and finally taking another ship up the coast of Mexico to San Francisco. It appears Charlie took the latter course and, after a rough twenty-two day passage from Panama, he finally arrived in San Francisco on 23rd June 1850.

Arriving in San Francisco today is one of the most exciting experiences in anyone's life but it was very different in 1850. Of course there was no Golden Gate Bridge to sail under and the 'city' was just a ramshackle shantytown. More worrying for Charlie was the disastrous news of the Glenmore and her cargo. Her backers were not alone in thinking they could make a fast buck from her cargo and a huge glut of tobacco had built up in the harbour. Prices were so low that the cargoes were simply left to rot on the quayside or pitched overboard into the harbour, adding to the general air of squalor and degradation, and the Glenmore was sold at a substantial loss. Needless to say the Virginia Company soon disbanded and from now on it was every man for himself.

However, Charlie was not one to be daunted by this set back and grabbing a pickaxe and shovel, he set off towards the gold fields.

Numerous tales surround Charlie's life and times in California - 'Charlie stories', as they are known. For these I am greatly indebted to William Sagar of the Fairfax Historical Society, whose collection of excerpts from books, articles and press reports are contained in his exhaustive work *More about Charles and Ada Fairfax,* published in 2004. Some of these stories are true and others quite likely fictitious, so we must take some of his supposed adventures with a pinch of salt. California was, after all, a wild and dangerous place so we should not be too surprised at some of the scrapes he found himself in and it was certainly a very different world to the one he left behind in Virginia. However, what they do show us is that he was quite a character and remembered affectionately long after his death.

Although his career as a gold prospector was to be short lived, he was not above getting his hands dirty and spent that first winter labouring away at Grass Valley in Yuba County with the mass of humanity drawn there in search of the elusive, life-changing nugget. Life in the gold fields was rough and tough, with fights over disputed claims a common occurrence. In his 1908 memoirs *Reminiscences of Senator William M Stewart of Nevada,* the author remembers Charlie Fairfax with a mule and cart hauling gravel to Deer Creek from the diggings on Coyote Hill. One day he got into an argument with another mule driver and a fight ensured. Charlie showed remarkable spirit and 'was willing to fight the whole party' much to the future senator's delight; from that moment on the two became firm friends and would remain allies in their future careers.

The work was hard and unrelenting: for the few who struck it lucky there were many more who did not. Charlie clearly fell into the latter category but if he found no gold he had at least began to build a reputation as a brave and honourable fellow and his popularity would grow and endure in the years to come. These qualities were in short supply in those pioneering days of the Golden West, where the pursuit of riches drove men to cheat and kill all too readily.

So what was Charlie to do? Gold mining was obviously not the answer and in any case he was not really cut out for that rough life; after all he had grown up on a plantation in Virginia with a pliable 'workforce' to do all the heavy lifting. In truth it really was not the life for a Virginian Gentleman. Charlie's real talent was with people and wherever he went he found new friends and admirers.

Moreover, the fact that he could by right call himself Lord Fairfax if he had so wished, did not go unnoticed and he was often referred to as 'The Baron', which doubtless added to his appeal.

So the answer to Charlie's dilemma became clear: if he could charm the birds out of the trees and command their respect too, then doubtless he could do the same with the voters. Politics it would be. One would like to think, given his background and the influence of his redoubtable parents, that a strong sense of civic duty was his overriding incentive. The fact that he might make a decent living from this 'trade' might just have been a reason too!

Charlie set about his new career with accustomed enthusiasm and his rise to political prominence was certainly meteoric. In 1851 he became a delegate for Yuba County to the Democratic State Convention and by 1852 had been elected as Justice of the Peace for the town of Marysville. Next he was elected as one of the county's two Associate Judges of the Court of Sessions, responsible for local administration and settling minor civic matters such as contract and mortgage disputes. By 1853 we find the ambitious young politician-in-the-making successfully running for the California State Assembly, where he represented Yuba and Sierra Counties. Re-elected the next year, he was appointed as Speaker of the House in Sacramento. This might have been enough for some men but not for Charlie, who in 1856 succeeded in getting himself elected as Clerk of the Supreme Court of California, a post he held until 1861, with the very handsome salary of $3,000 a year.

Much of Charlie's success could be put down to the fact that he was what we would today call a 'people person' - he loved the company of his fellow man and they loved him in return. Whenever there was a party or gathering, you would find Charlie there and always its life and soul. He would get involved in anything and everything, in fact you might say he was the original 'can-do' Californian – nothing is impossible and anything can be fun!

He also won many friends and admirers for his attitude to the key issue of the day, slavery, soon to tear the country apart. California had declared itself a free state and Charlie was more than happy to go along with that. Some might have imagined a gentleman planter from Virginia would have harboured the opposite view, but of course Charlie's grandfather, Thomas 9th Lord Fairfax, had been an early abolitionist so it comes as no surprise that he shared the same liberal sentiments.

All in all he was a natural choice for these important governmental posts, a charming, amusing and able man liked by all – well almost all. It might be added that Charlie was also a prominent freemason, something which may not have hindered his prospects either.

His life was not all work and when time allowed, Charlie took every opportunity to escape to the delights of San Francisco. One commentator has described him as, '*The Beau Brummel of San Francisco's Golden Dawn. He dressed in a brown velvet coat with lace ruffles on his shirt, when most men in those days wore stiffly starched white linen shirts, frock coats, silk hats, high boots and carried heavy guns in their belts. He had a mild, pleasant voice, his eyes were kind and always laughing: he was courteous, gallant, debonair, a charming gentleman when ladies were present...Charlie Fairfax was always a gentleman.'*

In an excerpt from her book *The Fantastic City, Memoirs of the Social and Romantic Life of Old San Francisco*, the author Amelia Ransome Neville paints a colourful picture of those early days: '*The grand social events of a season of the Fifties were the Apollo Balls. These were subscription parties given in Apollo Hall on Pacific Street, since then part of the notorious Barbary Coast....Apollo Hall was a bare loft with unfinished rafters which were hung with bunting for our dances. Wooden benches were the only seats, but they supported the wealth and fashion of San Francisco and many handsome gowns. A great beau was Charley Fairfax, of Virginia, the 'Baron' to all his friends since he actually was the heir to a title in England, although the family had lived for generations in America. He was Clerk in the Supreme Court at Sacramento, but commuted to San Francisco weekly or oftener, and was one of the early members of the Pacific Club, where his wit and good fellowship made him a favourite.'*

She goes on to recount an amusing story of how one day shortly before the Civil War, Charlie was sounding off to a group of fellow Southerners about the differences between them and those from the North. The 'Baron' delivered a scathing denunciation of the North and then turned to her father, who was always known as the 'Colonel' and assumed to be one of their kind. '*By the way, what part of the South are you from Colonel?*' he asked to reassure himself. '*Why,*' replied her father quietly, '*I'm from the southern part of Connecticut!*'

Not all these events were so civilised and on another occasion while running for Clerk of the Supreme Court, Charlie found himself in a brawl. The party laid into one another and Charlie, small as he was, found himself being tossed around like a feather on the backs of the belligerents.

Needless to say, he survived this encounter and it must have done little to hurt his popularity as he won the election.

It was probably at one of these gatherings that Charlie was to meet his wife, Ada Benham, a native of Cincinnati, where he had spent some time as a law student and quite possibly became acquainted with her family. Ada was considered quite a catch and there was something almost regal in her demeanour. Indeed, she came from a well to do family, whose grandfather Robert Benham, a Revolutionary War hero, had been among the founders of Cincinnati in 1790. Her father Joseph was a well-known attorney in Ohio and Kentucky, and her brother Calhoun Benham was then a rising force in San Francisco politics. Ada made an ideal partner for Charlie, as sparky and gregarious as himself and soon their thoughts turned to marriage. So early in 1855 they made the long journey back East, not as one might have imagined to her home town of Cincinnati, nor to Virginia, but to Louisville, Kentucky, where they were married in true Southern style on 10th January at the home of Ada's step-sister Henrietta and her husband George Prentice, a well-known local newspaper proprietor.

When the newlyweds eventually returned to San Francisco later in 1855, their first priority was of course to find somewhere to live and once again their luck was in: Charlie's old friend from Virginia, Dr Alfred Taliaferro, had settled in Marin County, just to the north of San Francisco, where he became the county's first resident physician. Here he gained the respect of the whole community and not least that of the local Mexican landowner, Don Domingo Sais. Don Domingo was a man of great importance in the county, with some 7,000 acres to his name, a reward for his efforts in helping Mexico gain its independence from Spain in 1839, long before California joined the Union. In 1851 he in turn gave 32 acres of land on Cascade Creek to Dr Taliaferro in recognition of his services to the community.

Charlie and Ada were frequent visitors to their friend's estate, where they revelled in the charms of the Marin countryside. Charlie would go hunting with his friend for deer, elk, bear and pheasant or would sit by the creek waiting for a fish to bite. Shortly after their return to California and to what must have been their great surprise and delight, Dr Taliaferro announced that he would make a gift of his land to them as a wedding present!

Charlie and Ada called their new home Bird's Nest Glen, a name that captured the beauty of its idyllic situation. Charlie's radiant bride made quite an impact on the citizens of Marin County. '*Her manners,*' reported one resident of the time, '*were those of a princess…and while people referred to her husband as Charlie, they referred to her only as Lady Fairfax*'.

Today, not much has changed since their time there. Although the original house was replaced long ago, the estate is still a verdant paradise, teeming with wildlife and when I visited with my family in 2002, deer came bounding across the paddock not more than twenty yards from where we stood. The creek burbles gently by and one can easily imagine Charlie and Ada strolling arm in arm through the beautiful grounds. The delightful small town that grew up around the property was incorporated in 1931 and named Fairfax in their memory, and it is an easy going, well-mannered place with a broad main street that sits comfortably in the valley.

Charlie and Ada loved their life at Bird's Nest Glen and made many improvements to their property, importing game birds to provide sport for hunting while Ada planted trees and flowers in profusion. Soon they became famous for their lavish 'Southern' hospitality, entertaining friend and stranger alike with copious quantities of food and drink. The story goes that Charlie would place bottles in the creek and then draw them up, nicely chilled, to the surprise and delight of his guests. All in all, it was a small paradise they happily shared with others.

If one gets the impression that Charlie's life was all 'beer and skittles' as the old English saying goes, it would only be partly true. Away from his bucolic rural life at Bird's Nest Glen, Charlie took his political duties seriously and was an assiduous servant of the State. Moreover, as we have seen, life in California was lived constantly on the brink and despite his elevated position, Charlie was not immune from sudden danger and the possibility of death, as one well-documented event reveals.

The truth is not everyone held Charlie in the high regard he could usually expect. In particular, he had made an enemy of a certain Harvey Lee, a reporter at the Supreme Court. Matters came to a head one day in 1858, when the two met outside the old St George Hotel in Sacramento. Some accounts say that Lee was drunk, but whatever the circumstances, a heated argument ensued and then quick as a flash, Lee pulled a sword from his walking cane and ran Charlie through just above the heart. Dropping to the ground Charlie summoned enough strength to pull out the pistol he always kept in his vest and pointed it at Lee. Then, instead of shooting his assailant, he dropped his gun and cried out: '*You are a braggart and a coward and you have killed me. But I spare your life, not for your sake, but for the sake of your wife and children.*' Luckily Charlie did not die but he lay perilously close to death for several weeks before he slowly began to recover, much to everyone's relief. Needless to say, Charlie's generous behaviour to his assailant was taken as another example of his 'gentlemanly' qualities and his reputation rose still further.

16. Distant Drums of War

Meanwhile, far away in the East the ominous drumbeat of war grew ever louder. Events were now spiralling out of control and soon the Southern slave-owning states would secede from the Union. Fort Sumter and all the bloody events of that dreadful conflict would follow, leaving many hundreds of thousands dead, maimed, widowed or orphaned.

California had been founded as a free state and was largely immune from the maelstrom that enveloped the eastern states. The State's main involvement in the war came in the form of valuable gold shipments that helped finance the Union's war effort, and the recruitment of volunteers. In all, by the war's end, as many as 17,000 men had rallied to the colours, the highest figure from any state. Not everyone was for the Union and many discreetly left to join the Southern cause. In California itself, while there was no open conflict to speak of, there were secessionist plots in the early stages of the war. However, these were small scale and easily quashed. General Sidney Albert Johnston, the Commander of Federal troops in California, strongly supported secession and he was seen as the rallying point for dissent. Although he did little other than voice his opinions, the authorities correctly doubted his loyalty and he was replaced in 1861 by General Edwin Sumner. This proved to be a wise decision, as Johnston fled across the Colorado River to Arizona where he joined the Confederate Army and was later killed leading his men at the Battle of Shiloh.

Others followed suit, including Charlie's brother-in-law Calhoun Benham, by this time the Attorney General of California. Benham had gained a certain notoriety for his role in the infamous 1859 duel between Senator David C. Broderick and David S. Terry, previously Chief Justice of the

Californian Supreme Court, which resulted in the death of the Senator.

A Southerner by birth and strong conviction, in November 1861 he quietly slipped aboard the steamship Oriziba together with two fellow prominent Southern sympathisers, Senator William Gwin and Senator J. L. Brent. Although we cannot be entirely sure of their intentions, we do know they were carrying important papers which they hoped would benefit the Confederacy.

Their secret mission soon turned to farce when, in an episode worthy of a Hollywood comedy, the conspirators realised they had chosen to travel on a ship that was also carrying the military commander of California, General Sumner, and 500 Union troops! Word soon reached the General there were three suspicious characters on board and when they reached Panama they were abruptly arrested for making 'treasonable utterances'. Luckily for them, Senator Gwin had just enough time to throw the carpet bag containing the vital papers out of the porthole and thus saved them from a traitor's fate.

After incarcerating them for a while in New York, and without any firm evidence of their treasonous intentions, the authorities had no choice but to release them. Calhoun Benham went south to join the Confederate Army where he served under Major General Patrick Cleburne, the 'Stonewall of the West' and hero of Missionary Ridge. Unlike his commanding officer, he survived the war and eventually returned to California. Senator Brent lived out his days In Maryland and Senator Gwin also came back to California where he died.

Events now took a turn for the worse in Charlie's life. In the Presidential election of 1860 the Democratic Party fell apart, with one faction nominating the Southern sympathiser John C. Breckinridge for President and the other the Northern Democrat Stephen A. Douglas. This allowed Abraham Lincoln's Republican Party to sweep the board, and would lead to the secession of the Southern States and Civil War. Likewise in California, the Democrats lost heavily to the Republicans, led by Leland Stanford, a tough no-nonsense figure and close ally of Lincoln. Stanford was largely responsible for keeping California out of the War and his reward was the franchise to build the western section of the transcontinental railroad. This made him and his associates a vast fortune, and earned them the nickname 'The Big Four'. Others called them 'Robber Barons' for obvious reasons. Later on in life he would put some of his immense fortune to good use and found Stanford University. Of course the change in administration spelt the end for the Democrat Charlie's lucrative job as Clerk to the Supreme Court, and with it his political career.

Then came terrible news from Virginia: Vaucluse, the family home near Alexandria, was no more. The Federal Government in Washington, terrified at the approaching Confederate Army just across the Potomac, hastily threw up a ring of defensive forts around the capitol. Vaucluse, located on a hill just three miles from Alexandria, was an obvious place for one of these. The house was raised to the ground and the members of the Fairfax family still living there, his aunt and two cousins, fled to safety in Richmond. For the next five years, the war would rage around the old Fairfax demesne and throughout what had once been the Northern Neck Proprietary, so there was no possibility of Charlie going back to his old home, even if he had wanted to.

One might well ask why Charlie did not join the other Southerners and rush to the colours? Perhaps his position is best explained in Charlie's own words, reported by his friend Stephen J. Field, who later became an Associate Justice of the Supreme Court of America: '*Though I am a Virginian by birth, I have adopted California, and whilst I live in a State which has taken her hand with the Northern people, I cannot in honour do anything, and I will not, to weaken her attachment to the Union. If my health were good, I should leave the State and return to Virginia and give my services to her; but, as that is impossible, I shall remain in California, and, whilst here, will not be false to her by anything I do or say.'*

This statement tells us much about Charlie's innate sense of honour and loyalty to his adopted State. More to the point, Charlie's health had been severely weakened by the vicious attack he had suffered and his appetite for a drink did little to improve matters. Whatever the case, he was certainly in no position to fight.

Perhaps one of the most extraordinary ideas for his future came from a very remarkable figure in California's early days, Bishop William Kip. A New Yorker by birth, Kip had been appointed the Episcopal Missionary Bishop to California in 1853. His records of those days provide a remarkable account of life in the Golden West and there are several mentions of Charlie Fairfax. In 1860, Kip travelled to England where he was entertained by the Marquess of Hertford. At a gathering of 'Nobles High in Government', Kip told them of the curious case of the English nobleman who had settled in California. A few days later, Lord Hertford met the Bishop again when he told him:

> *'Lord D. . . . (who was one of Her Majesty's ministers) was extremely interested in your description of Charles Fairfax the other night at dinner and he consulted with a number of his friends of both parties. We consider it a great loss to England that so illustrious a title should be lost, and he desired me to convey the information to Charles Fairfax through you, that he may be assured the restoration of Leeds Castle and sufficient property to maintain him as befits his rank if he will take up his dwelling place and title in England.'*

This was a truly extraordinary and generous suggestion which must have seemed fantastical to the Virginia planter's son turned Californian pioneer. Britain and its aristocracy were a world entirely alien to Charlie, as the Fairfax family had been American citizens for as long as the country had been established and colonists long before that. Such an offer, even from members of the British Government and Parliament, must have seemed entirely unrealistic. Charlie may have been a romantic but he was certainly not mad; so, true to his country and adopted State, he rejected this rather eccentric idea out of hand and nothing more was heard of it. However, there is an interesting footnote to this story.

Although we cannot be sure of the identity of 'Lord D', it is my guess that he was the 1st Marquess of Dufferin & Ava, great diplomat of Queen Victoria's reign and variously Ambassador to Paris, Constantinople and St. Petersburg, Governor-General of Canada and Viceroy of India. The reason for my conjecture is that Lord Dufferin is quoted in Constance Burton Harrison's 1888 history of the Fairfax family, bemoaning their loss to America: *'All Englishmen who love their country wish that the Fairfax title had remained where it belongs. It is the lost Pleiad of the British Galaxy.'* This is a reference to Greek mythology where 'the Lost Pleiad' refers to Merope, the youngest of the seven Pleiades, the daughters of Zeus, who married Sisyphus. On becoming mortal, she faded away.

This interest in the Fairfax's is quite a coincidence. If I am right in my identification of 'Lord D', then Lord Dufferin would have been very pleased to know that his great-granddaughter, Sonia, would one day marry Charlie's great nephew, Thomas 13th Lord Fairfax – our mother and father!

17. The Duel at Bird's Nest Glen

In that fateful year of 1861, an infamous event took place at Bird's Nest Glen that provides a vivid illustration of the passions aroused by the dreadful conflict between the North and South.

Daniel Showalter and Charles Piercy had known each other since childhood and had once been friends; they had travelled to California together and both had shown early promise as representatives of their counties in the State Legislature (Mariposa and San Bernadino respectively). But now they were fierce political rivals. Although both were Democrats, after the party split, Showalter, a Southerner by birth, naturally sided with the Southern faction, while Piercy went with the Northern. Relations between the two got steadily worse and finally came to a head when they competed for election as Speaker of the House in 1861. Insults were traded and each questioned the other's honour. Such a matter was taken very seriously in those days and, according to the 'Code Duello', there was only one way it could be settled!

The day for the duel was set but the news had leaked out. In order to avoid the attention of the Sheriff, the two men, with their seconds and followers, rode out on horseback to Bird's Nest Glen, then still a fairly remote and discreet location. Charlie knew both men well and ever the diplomat, did his best to persuade them to abandon their plan. He knew that the likely outcome of the duel would be the death of one or both and it was not in his nature to encourage such murderous recklessness. Despite the strained atmosphere, Charlie and Ada laid on a fine lunch for the protagonists and their supporters, all the while hoping he could prevail upon them to see sense. However, his best efforts were in vain, and not long after lunch the two parties made their way to a meadow some way from Charlie and Ada's property. The men were armed with rifles, so it was a foregone conclusion that one would be killed – in effect murdered – and so it was. Piercy fell to the ground, shot through the head, and died instantly.

Showalter, by all accounts a dislikeable character, was duly indicted by the Marin County Grand Jury for the murder, but he never did come to trial. Fleeing with a band of Southern sympathisers eager to join the fight against the Yankees, he too met his end within a month. Somewhere in the Arizona desert, the party was ambushed, possibly by Apaches or white outlaws, and only a handful escaped. It is said Showalter fought bravely, but against the overwhelming odds, they stood no chance.

Could Charlie have done more to stop these young hot heads from their rash action? Perhaps he could or should have - after all, he still held high State office at the time and it was his civic duty to uphold the law. However, in those wild times, a duel was considered a nobler way for gentlemen to settle disagreements than a lawsuit. In the end, both men died and nothing was gained by their violent ends. The old saying that 'pride comes before a fall' was as true as ever in this case.

18. The Shadows Lengthen

If life was now quieter for Charlie on the public front, his wife made sure things were seldom quiet at home. Under Ada's sway, the fame of their legendary open-house policy had by now spread far and wide. Such was the couple's generosity that on summer Sundays, scores of revellers would drive out from San Rafael and enjoy their hospitality. It seems there was no limit to the numbers they entertained and as one put it, their house 'was like an omnibus – always room for one more.' Charlie and Ada had truly created a west coast version of life in the ante-bellum South. One man remembered it as a child: *'Farmers, cattlemen, even strangers never passed the Fairfax residence. A great table was always spread out and at the noon meal, what with the regulars and the casuals, it took on the appearance of a vast boarding house. In those days the cost of living didn't worry anyone. Fruit, vegetables, milk, butter, fish, game were all at hand. The price of beef and mutton was a joke. Labour cost nothing as there were a lot of loose characters who preferred to hang around the Fairfax home and work for their keep, rather than earn wages elsewhere.'*

But the truth was that Charlie was no longer the dashing young blade at the forefront of Californian life he had once been. He had never really recovered from the wound he received on the street corner in Sacramento and now people were beginning to notice that his drinking was becoming rather more than just a social pleasure. However, he did not drop entirely out of sight and when the Civil War ended, he was narrowly elected to the rather modest role of County Supervisor for the First District of Marin County.

It was in this year that Charlie and Ada made what was to be their only venture into the world of business. Going into partnership with one James Dixon, they bought a saw mill at Fort Ross, eighteen miles north of Bodega Bay, on a stretch of tableland high above the Pacific. Fort Ross had been established by Russian fur trappers in the early 1800s and was still a wooden stockade. The idea was to harvest the giant redwood trees that grew in profusion along the coast, to supply the expanding market for high-quality timber.

As it turned out Charlie never did become a logger, for in 1868 he was elected chairman of the ten-man delegation to the Democratic National Convention in New York. So in June of that year he bade farewell to California for what would turn out to be the last time.

As had been widely expected, the great hero of the Union Army, the Republican Ulysses S. Grant, swept all before him in the subsequent presidential election, leaving the Democrats utterly defeated. It looked like his political career was over and Charlie left New York for a long delayed reunion with his mother Caroline and his brother Dr John Contee Fairfax, in Washington DC.

Although his mother was now sixty-two years old, Charlie seemed older. His health was ruined and wracked with tuberculosis, his condition grew worse over the winter months. By the beginning of 1869, Charlie lay dying. The Marin County Journal of 27th February carried this report:

> *A correspondent of the Times, writing from Washington DC under the date of January 20th writes as follows in relation to the health of Charles S. Fairfax who is now lying ill in that city:*
>
> *'I have heretofore endeavoured to stave off a report of his declining health in hopes that a change for the better might take place: but his gradual sinking and inability to receive nourishment constrains me to say that his numerous friends in California may prepare for the worst at any time.'*

Ada went east to be with him in his final days and arrived just in time, for on Sunday, 4th April, Charles Snowden

Fairfax, rightful 10th Lord Fairfax of Cameron, passed away. He was just forty.

There is a remarkable anecdote told of Charlie's passing and whether it is true or not, we cannot be certain. However, the fact that it has been recorded at all gives the story some credibility: the doctor called to examine Charlie's body was staggered to find that the wound he had sustained eleven or so years before in Sacramento was still as fresh as the day he had received it – an extraordinary medical phenomenon.

The sad news of Charlie's death reached California in well under twenty-four hours, thanks to the new telegraph line along the route of the soon-to-be-completed Transcontinental Railroad. His obituary in the Sacramento Union newspaper went as follows:

> *'Charlie is dead. At last he had to yield to the King of Terrors. The struggle was long and painful. Fairfax died at the residence of his mother, sixteen miles from Washington, on Sunday last. His body was brought into the City on Tuesday and was met at the Baltimore (and Ohio) depot by a large number of Californians, who joined in the procession from Rock Creek Church, six miles from Georgetown, where the funeral took place in accordance with the forms of the Episcopal Church and the Masonic Fraternity. The body is deposited in the vault of a relative for a time, the laws of Maryland not allowing a corpse to be taken out of the State until a certain time has elapsed after decease. Ultimately the remains are to be interred on the estate in Virginia. Rock Creek Church is one of the oldest in the United States. The bricks of which it is constructed were brought from England.'*

So ends the tale of Charlie Fairfax, the Virginian of noble English blood who made California his home and is fondly remembered to this day as that most attractive of characters - the ebullient, generous host and friend to all.

The distinguished jurist Stephen J. Field wrote in his *Personal Reminiscences of Early California*, '*No man in the State was more popular.*'

'*He was the life and soul of every company into which he was cast,*' wrote another in the San Francisco Daily Evening Post, who added, '*He was alike at home in the drawing room or the mountain miner's camp.*' Journalist James W. Wilkins wrote: '*Anyone with half an eye could see Fairfax was a gentleman by right. He had a bearing, poise, an unconscious stateliness that is born, not made.*'

What of Charlie's widow, the formidable Ada? Whatever else, she could rise to any challenge and she soon returned to California. Bird's Nest Glen was not the same without Charlie, so she sold it and moved to Fort Ross, where her husband's partner James Dixon was running the logging business he and Charlie had bought together. Although entirely unprepared for this new life, she quickly adapted to her role as a business woman. She also resumed her role as a gracious hostess and, as in the Bird's Nest Glen days, all were welcome at her door. However, the business was never able to support Ada's extravagant lifestyle and when Dixon was killed in a log jam only three years later, she sold Fort Ross too.

Ada's later years were spent in Washington DC where, possibly on the strength of her reputation for boundless hospitality, she was became the 'Official Hostess' at the White House. Her role was to act as First Lady to the bachelor President Grover Cleveland and host official receptions for visiting dignitaries. How fitting for the Belle of Bird's Nest Glen!

Ada passed away in 1888, and is buried beside her husband in Rock Creek Cemetery.

The tradition of hospitality started by Charles and Ada at Bird's Nest Glen continued in the years ahead. The property became a popular picnic spot for San Franciscans in the

1880s and on one occasion three thousand assembled in what was described as 'one grand drunken shindy'. By 1905, the property had been acquired by Charles and Adele Pastori, he a famous chef and she a former opera singer, and they opened a celebrated restaurant there. Although Charlie and Ada's original house burnt down in 1911, the Pastoris rebuilt the restaurant and remained in business until 1925. Legend has it that Irving Berlin would serenade diners on a piano hoisted high in a tree! Many of their guests would have been the stars of early Hollywood, as the rugged location was a favourite with producers for making low-budget Westerns. Later still, the property became the Marin Town and Country Club, until it closed in 1972.

We are lucky enough still to possess, a century and a half later, a wonderful souvenir of Charlie's adventures in California. I have it here in front of me – it is a solid gold pocket watch given to him on the day he left California. Lift the cover and these words are clearly inscribed:

'Hon. Chas S. Fairfax from his California Friends May 1868'.

Part 4. Civil War

19. The Connection

With the death of Charlie Fairfax, his brother Dr John Contee Fairfax now inherited the right to style himself Lord Fairfax. As with Charlie, John had no interest in this ancient British title and was always known simply as Dr John Contee Fairfax. Quite different in character to his buccaneering brother, John attended the University of Pennsylvania where he qualified as a doctor and in 1857 he married Mary Kirby. The world they now lived in was very different from that which Charlie had left behind. The genteel life of the old South was now just a distant memory, shattered by the cataclysmic events of the Civil War, and the Fairfax family were no longer even Virginians.

The experience of the Fairfax family during the war was no harder than that of many other Southern families. Indeed, many had it much worse. But before we embark upon those dark times, let us first of all return to those long-lost days before the war and catch a glimpse of the charmed life they had lost. Fortunately for us, Dr John's cousin Constance Burton Harrison was an avid chronicler of her times and in her 1911 book *Recollections Grave and Gay* she paints a vivid picture of her youth at the old family home, Vaucluse, before the war.

Constance (1843-1920) was the daughter of Monimia, the youngest daughter of Thomas 9th Lord Fairfax, who had married Archibald Cary of Cumberland, Maryland. A great-nephew of Thomas Jefferson, Archibald's father, Wilson Jefferson Cary and his bride Miss Virginia Randolph were married at Monticello. The bride was given away by the grand old man himself and he presented her with a pearl necklace, especially ordered from Paris.

After her husband's death in 1854, Monimia took her three children, Falkland, Constance and Clarence to live with her elderly widowed mother, Margaret Fairfax, at Vaucluse, high up on a ridge above Alexandria. Vaucluse had originally been built by Valentine Peyton on a 50,000-acre plantation, long since broken up, and was named after the location of Petrarch's house in Avignon, France. For a while it was home to George Washington's doctor, Dr James Craik, before Thomas 9th Lord Fairfax purchased the house in the 1820s. It was here that Charlie and Dr John had been born, although both had long since fled the nest. Dr John was now living with his mother and stepfather William Sanders at Woodburn, their home near Washington, while Charlie was making hay in California. So, the arrival of Monimia and her brood was far from unwelcome, indeed it was encouraged. Constance tells us there was a continual flow of family members in and out of Vaucluse, and these became known as 'The Connection'. Anyone connected by birth or marriage was always welcome there, the physical and spiritual home of the extended Fairfax clan.

Constance's descriptions of life at Vaucluse are unique and immensely valuable, providing a window into that lost ante-bellum world, which, like the house, had long gone. The house itself was an old, white stucco building with wings on either side, framed by great oak trees that stood on the lawn in front. There were stables and a dwelling for the coloured servants. Constance makes it quite clear that these servants were hired, not slaves, and takes great pride in pointing out that her grandfather had been among the first in Virginia to free or 'manumit' his slaves long before the abolition movement gained widespread support.

Although there was no farm attached to the place, there were gardens, a chicken yard, an orchard and a dairy to supply the house with all its needs. The house itself was a treasure trove of Fairfax family possessions, collected from old family houses in England and Virginia - Belvoir, Toulston and Ash Grove. There were portraits of a 'Parliamentary General' and a Lady Fairfax in a busk with a feather in her hand. These were probably of the celebrated English Civil War General, Sir Thomas Fairfax and his wife. There were others, and quite possibly among them are those that now hang in our homes in England.

The drawing room was large and bright, with big windows that flooded the room with light, all beautifully furnished and curtained with crimson damask. Logs crackled in the large hearth all winter, and on the shelves there were quantities of dusty ancient books and manuscripts relating to the Fairfax family, some even dating back to the time of Richard the Lionheart! Among them were displayed an assortment of ostrich eggs and many fine pieces of Dresden china, all which added to the homely feel – one can well imagine the welcoming scene.

Constance's childhood was clearly happy and carefree. Surrounded by so many young male cousins of all ages, she was something of a tomboy, climbing trees, riding the horses and generally roughing it. Her only female cousin, the widowed Aunt Eugenia's daughter, Meta Hyde, she seems to have held in some contempt, contrasting with her admiration for her male cousins.

In time a French governess, Mademoiselle Adami, was engaged to instil in this reluctant tomboy a sense of feminine decorum and under her tutelage she gained a love of the French language that would last throughout her life. Shopping expeditions to Washington, only eight miles away, were a highlight of these years and her descriptions of these give us a wonderful picture of life in those golden days before the War. The shopping party would travel in the family coach drawn by *two highly groomed chestnuts with long frizzled tails in which we jogged over the Long Bridge to have our daguerrotypes taken at Whitehurst's, to order bonnets of Miss Wilson, and to eat ices at Gautier's.'*

There was much chat among the grown-ups about the goings-on at Queen Victoria's court, a constant source of fascination for these ladies of English descent. There was also constant gossip about members of Washington's society, to nearly all of whom they seem to have been related. Gradually the talk began to take on a more sombre tone as the slide to war began to gather pace. No one wanted secession and the question on everyone's lips was what Colonel Robert E. Lee would do.

Sometimes the girls would stay in Washington with another of her mother's sisters, Aurelia, her husband James Irwin, and their two children Orlando and Augusta. Constance tells us that it was from their house that she would leave several years later for her first Washington ball. On other occasions they would visit her much-loved uncle Dr Orlando Fairfax and his wife Mary at Fairfax House on Cameron Street, Alexandria. Their son Randolph would be killed at the Battle of Fredericksburg, a tragedy that was to be repeated in so many homes across the land. It was here also that Constance would be held under house arrest during the dark days of the war.

Constance was keenly aware of the Fairfax family's distinguished history both in America and England. At times she writes poignantly about the lives of those long departed and the houses they occupied. She visits Belvoir, the seat of Colonel William Fairfax and by then an overgrown ruin, wishing that it could be restored to its former glory. Writing in 1911, Constance tells us that her son Fairfax Harrison, a successful businessman and later President of the Southern Railroad Company, had built his own version of the house in Fauquier County and named it Belvoir. Prized among his possessions was a copy of Thoresby's *Antiquities of Yorkshire*, which he had acquired from the antiquarian collector B. F. Stevens in London. Inscribed on its fly leaf were the signatures of those distinguished visitors to Belvoir in its heyday, together with the signatures of some modern members of the family, including our grandfather Albert, the 12th Lord. The book had apparently been taken to England by George William Fairfax and sold after his death.

These early years were interrupted by two sad events. First, in 1856, her beloved elder brother and the apple of his mother's eye, Falkland, died suddenly at the age of just sixteen. He had just started work and high hopes rested on his young shoulders, so his death was a bitter blow particularly to his mother, who, as Constance tells us, never really recovered from his loss. Two years later her grandmother Margaret Fairfax, widow of Thomas 9th Lord, passed away at the age of seventy-five, thus severing the last link with the days when the Fairfax family held sway over Virginia society.

At this juncture, Constance makes an interesting observation which helps to shed a light on the future fortunes of the family. Ownership of Vaucluse now passed to Thomas and Margaret's eldest son, Constance's Uncle Reginald Fairfax. Constance tells us that the 9th Lord had left his surviving children a sizeable fortune and Reginald, despite serving in the Confederate Navy, had somewhat surprisingly, but wisely as it turned out, invested his inheritance in Federal bonds. When Reginald succumbed to malaria in 1862, Constance's mother Monimia was the lucky beneficiary of this shrewd investment decision, enabling her family to live in some considerable comfort. In sharp contrast, his brother Dr Orlando Fairfax had, like most loyal Southerners, invested his inheritance in Confederate bonds with predictably ruinous results.

Now in her teens, Constance was sent to a boarding school in Richmond run by a Monsieur Hubert Pierre

Lefebvre, which appears to have been a popular destination for the daughters of wealthy Southerners. Although she does not dwell much on these years, she was clearly unimpressed by her fellow pupils and makes the interesting observation that *'the surrounding slave service was inspiring neither to the energy of body nor independence of ideas I had been taught to consider indispensable. Many of these pretty languid creatures of the far Southern States had never put on a shoe or stocking for themselves; and the point of view of some about owning or chastising fellow beings who might chance to offend them was abhorrent to me. But they all came out grandly during the war, and after it.'* The influence of her enlightened grandfather Thomas Fairfax, devotee of Swedenborg and early advocate of emancipation, was clearly strong and she had inherited his loathing of slavery. Avidly she read Harriet Beecher Stowe's Uncle Tom's Cabin and when the news of John Brown's raid at Harper's Ferry arrived in Virginia, she records that she was *'inwardly terrified, because I thought it was God's vengeance for the torture of such as Uncle Tom.'* She could not know, or she would have been horrified there would be far, far worse to come.

20. Gone with the Wind

If you have ever seen that wonderfully romantic film *Gone with the Wind*, you will remember the scene near the beginning when all the young blades, whooping and hollering, jump on their horses and ride away to join the fight against those 'Damn Yankees'. In a scene that must have been repeated all over the South, Constance tells us that all the young men of the 'Connection' – fourteen or fifteen of them - did just that and eagerly rushed to join up. Vaucluse would obviously be in the line of fire, so her mother Monimia and her aunt Eugenia decided to send the younger ones away to a place of safety. Constance, her younger brother Clarence, and her cousin Meta Hyde were swiftly packed off to stay with relations at Millwood in Clarke County. Monimia was clearly well-informed and fully aware of the appalling suffering of the troops in the recent Crimean War. Taking their lead from the celebrated 'Lady with the Lamp', Florence Nightingale, she and Eugenia hurried to Manassas Junction where Confederate troops were now rallying for the fray. The ladies knew all too well that their services would soon be in demand.

Before she left Vaucluse, Monimia made a decision that would be of immense value to the family later on. Fearing the worst, she collected all the family silver together, sealed it in wooden boxes, buried it deep under the cellar and covered her tracks with piles of rubbish. As things turned out, the fate of this fine old house was far worse that Monimia or anyone could have guessed. The defeat of the Union Army of the Potomac at the First Battle of Manassas (or Bull Run as it is known in the North) in July 1861 sent panic through the high command and the Union's Commander-in-Chief, General McClellan, ordered a ring of forts to be built around the Capital. Vaucluse, perfectly sited, with views in all directions, was the obvious choice for one of these. Without further ado,

Union soldiers set about its destruction, commanded by Generals Horatio Wright and John Newton. A rough blockhouse named Fort Worth was built in its place and no one would ever have known that there had once stood the beautiful Fairfax family home. Constance adds that when the soldiers arrived they were very surprised to find two ladies, elderly Fairfax relations, still in the house, either too shocked or too frightened to move. Gently they were lifted onto a wagon and carried away to safety. Apart from the silver buried safely underground, everything else was lost. Truly it had all 'gone with the wind'.

There is at least a happy epilogue to this otherwise sad story: when the war was over and the fort cleared away, Constance and her mother Monimia returned with some men to where their house had once stood, in search of the buried treasure. After two days of digging and prodding nothing could be found, and they began to think the silver must have been found by the Yankees. Then, just as they were on the verge of giving up, a tea spoon, 'as black as jet', emerged! Feverishly they dug down and there it was, just as Monimia had left it all those years before, albeit considerably worse for wear. Packed off to Galt's in Washington (a well-known store of the time), the silver was soon restored to its former glory and 'pristine brilliancy'. I am pleased to add that some of this silver is still in use by the family today.

Today, a modern apartment block stands on the old house's commanding position, with views stretching miles into the far distance and it is easy to see why they chose to build a fort there. When I visited the site of Vaucluse in 2012, I found no trace of the old house or its gardens. But on moonlit nights it is said the ghostly figure of a young Confederate soldier can sometimes be seen, his light grey tunic stained with blood. The legend goes that he was shot by a Union picket while seeking out his sweetheart and where he stood, sweet smelling violets sprout from the soil…

Constance was to experience many ups and downs throughout the war, and she achieved fame as a journalist in Richmond, capital of the Confederate States, writing under the pen name of 'Refugitta'. Together with her two Cary cousins, Hetty and Jennie, she sewed the first examples of the Confederate flag and they were given the nickname the 'Cary Invincibles'. At one point she made a daring visit to Washington across the lines and was held under house arrest for a few days under suspicion as a spy, until she was allowed to return south. With her mother Monimia she worked as a nurse at Camp Winder, a harrowing experience for all concerned. Finally, she met and fell for her future husband, Burton Harrison, Private Secretary to Confederate President Jefferson Davis. Their relationship was not without difficulty, for at the War's end, he was among the Confederate leaders rounded up and imprisoned in Fort Delaware. In the bitter and vengeful atmosphere following the assassination of President Abraham Lincoln, their fate for a time looked very grim and it was two long years before Harrison was finally released. They married in 1867 and went on to enjoy a happy and prosperous life in New York and Bar Harbour, Maine, he a lawyer and she a successful writer.

21. Total War

Unlike the North, the experience of war in the South was all-encompassing and more devastating. Being less populous and less industrialised, the Confederacy had to mobilise every man and boy it could. It is shocking to discover that even Constance's fifteen-year-old brother Clarence was called to arms, enlisted as a 'marker' in an Alexandria regiment. Looking back on the conflict at a distance of over 150 years it is clear now that the South never really stood a chance. The South had a free white population of only 5.6 million against the North's 21.7 million and every other statistic shows it was at a clear disadvantage: 90% of all manufactured items and 97% of all firearms were made in the North, which also had a far more extensive rail system and telegraph network. However, in one respect the South seemed to have an advantage at the outset and that was in terms of exports. Before the War nearly 70% of all United States exports came from the Southern states, but of course this largely consisted of cotton and when the blockade of Southern ports took hold this trade rapidly collapsed. When its chief port, New Orleans, fell in 1862 the Confederacy's eventual defeat became inevitable. It was only because of the ingenuity and bravery of the blockade runners, together with the remarkable fighting spirit of its men, led by such outstanding generals as Thomas 'Stonewall' Jackson and Robert E. Lee, that the South held out for so long.

Only two major battles were fought in Union territory, Antietam in Maryland and Gettysburg in Pennsylvania, while all the others were fought on Southern soil or in the West. The average Southern soldier was a country boy, skilled on a horse and fiercely loyal to his State - it was, after all, 'States Rights' rather than slavery itself that caused the South to secede, and the emancipation of slavery did not become the official war aim of the Union until 1863. The

Northern soldier by contrast, was likely to come from a town or city and many were Irish immigrants, marched straight off the boat to the front. This is not to decry the spirit of the Northern soldier, many of whom doubtless abhorred slavery, but their chief inspiration came from a desire to preserve the Union.

The defining aspect of the war was the colossal scale of the casualties. Although the exact number of deaths has never been finally agreed, most experts give the figure of 620,000 from both sides, although some maintain it exceeded 700,000. Whatever the number, the slaughter was truly dreadful and far exceeded the combined totals of every war the United States has ever undertaken, from the Revolution to Vietnam and the more recent campaigns in the Middle East.

In many ways this was the first major war of the industrial age, where the railroad, steamship, telegraph and the mass-produced repeating rifle played a significant part. Tactics on the other hand, at least until near the end, resembled those employed by Napoleon and Wellington at the beginning of the 19th century. Battles were fought in drawn-up formation with predictably horrific results, with line upon line of infantry and cavalry mown down as they marched towards the guns. It was not until 1864 that we begin to see a more 'modern' and ruthless form of warfare emerge: Sherman's notorious 'March to the Sea', which involved the wholesale destruction of a large swathe of Georgia, and Grant's use of trench warfare at the Siege of Petersburg would foreshadow the horrors to come in the First World War, fifty years later.

There could have been few families in the South that that did not escape the heartbreak of losing a son and the Fairfax family was no exception. As we have heard, Constance's favourite uncle, Lieutenant Reginald Fairfax, died during the war, and although his death serving in the Confederate Navy was from malaria, it was as painful and sad to her as if it had been in battle. However, it was another of her uncles, Dr Orlando Fairfax, who would have to bear the loss of a son in battle. Reginald, aged just eighteen, was clearly the apple of his parent's eyes and a photograph we have of him shows a very handsome young man, dressed in his simple light grey uniform. This brave and much admired young man was a private in the Rockridge Artillery and clearly destined for great things. Members of his company would frequently say of him: 'What a good soldier Fairfax is!' But tragically, and like so many others, his promise was never fulfilled, for he fell at the Battle of Fredericksburg, cut down at dusk by a shell fragment while standing by his cannon. His body was brought to Richmond and placed on a bier in front of the altar of St James's Church, dressed in the same smoke-blackened, coarse flannel shirt he had worn in battle. When asked if he would like his son dressed in a clean uniform Dr Orlando replied, 'No. Let my son sleep his long sleep as he fell at the post of duty.' Later he was buried at Hollywood cemetery, his coffin draped with the flag for which he had fought.

In a moving tribute from the very highest level, Robert E. Lee found time to write these heartfelt words to his old friend Orlando Fairfax:

> *'I have grieved most deeply at the death of your noble son. I have watched his conduct from the commencement of the war and have pointed with pride to the patriotism, self-denial and manliness of character he has exhibited. I had hoped that an opportunity would have occurred for the promotion he deserved; not that it would have elevated him, but have shown that his devotion to duty was appreciated by his country. Such an opportunity would undoubtedly have occurred; but he has been translated to a better world, for which his purity and piety have eminently fitted him. You do not require to be told how great his gain. It is the living for whom I sorrow. I beg that you offer to Mrs Fairfax and your daughters, my heartfelt sympathy, for I know the depth of their grief.*

That God may give you and them the strength to bear this great affliction, is the earnest prayer of your early friend.'

R.E. Lee

28th December 1862.

22. The Good Doctor

I had rather despaired of having anything interesting to say about the good doctor from Maryland, John Contee, 11th Lord Fairfax, until a chance encounter one day not so long ago. We have always spent our summers on the Isle of Wight and when the father of an old friend died, I took the ferry over for the Service of Thanksgiving. Gathered at the family home afterwards, I was introduced to an elderly gentleman, Giles Mills, who, it emerged was a cousin from Maryland – although he, like me, had been born British. This was a delightful surprise and Giles's knowledge of our families' intertwined histories in Maryland was immensely valuable. As it has turned out our meeting was also very timely, for Giles, who had served with distinction in the Second World War, later becoming a General in the British Army and Governor of the Tower of London, sadly passed away not long after. Had I not attended the service that day, I might still have been in the dark about my great-grandfather's life and the interesting times he shared with Giles's forebears, his cousins in Maryland.

John Contee had been born in 1830 at Vaucluse, but when his father Albert Fairfax died in 1835, his mother Caroline Snowden Fairfax remarried Colonel William Sanders and from then onwards the family lived at Woodburn in Sandy Spring, Maryland, not far from Washington DC. So, from an early age John was a Marylander rather than a Virginian and would remain so all his life. Here he grew up surrounded by his Snowden cousins and was undeniably closer to them than to his Fairfax relations in Virginia.

The Snowdens, as we know, were a prominent Maryland family whose wealth derived from iron working in the 18th century. Their principal home, Montpelier, near Laurel in

Prince George's County, Maryland, is a fine Palladian mansion. It still stands today and it was there that Caroline was born. Her parents, Richard Snowden and Eliza (née Warfield), had seven children, five of whom reached maturity and it is from them that we and the late General Giles Mills descend.

Giles was descended from Caroline's younger sister Emily Roseville Snowden, a great beauty who married General T.P. Andrews of Baltimore, a distinguished veteran of the Mexican-American War of 1846-48. As we shall see, two of their children, a daughter also named Emily Roseville and her son Richard Snowden Andrews, would feature dramatically in the life of my great-grandfather, their cousin Dr John Contee.

After Dr John had qualified as a doctor at the University of Pennsylvania he returned to Maryland and set up practice at his mother's house, Woodburn. Medicine in those days was a primitive business and the danger of germs entirely unknown. In particular, childbirth was extremely hazardous and many women died due to 'puerperal fever'. Doctors now know that this is a bacterial infection which leads to puerperal sepsis, an extreme form of septicaemia and usually results in a painful death for the mother. At the time it was thought that it was caused by contagion like yellow fever, while of course it was actually caused by lack of hygiene. Although by this time some research had begun to point to the need for cleanliness, the medical orthodoxy clung to its old beliefs with many tragic results.

Such a tragedy befell Dr John's cousin, Emily Roseville Andrews, who was overjoyed when in 1858 she was due again. Dr John was very fond of her and as there had been an 'outbreak of puerperal fever' (or so it was thought) in Baltimore, he sent for her to have the baby in his own home. This was a very kind gesture as his own wife was expecting and it was then thought that the disease was infectious. Sadly poor Emily Roseville died just two weeks later, quite unnecessarily, but of course no one then knew any better. Her little daughter Emily Rosalie Snowden Marshall was raised by her grandparents in Baltimore and would grow up to marry Judge Somerville Pinkney Tuck, later US Ambassador to Egypt and director of the Suez Canal Company.

Her widowed husband Charles Marshall, holding the rank of Colonel, served in the Civil War as Military Secretary to General Robert E. Lee and drafted many of his despatches and orders, including the poignant Field Order No. 9, 'Farewell to the Army of Northern Virginia.' In the well-known picture of the end of the War, we can see the defeated Confederate General mounted on his famous horse 'Traveller', riding slowly away from the surrender at Appomattox Court House with Colonel Marshall at his side, the only officer to be present on that solemn day.

After the war Colonel Marshall remarried, to a cousin of his first wife Sarah Snowden, the daughter of Colonel Thomas Snowden, and resumed his law practice in Baltimore. As a footnote it is worth mentioning that his nephew, George C. Marshall, would achieve greatness in his lifetime as Chief of Staff of the United States Army in the Second World War. Later, as Secretary of State, he was the author of the Marshall Plan which brought about the resurrection of Europe from the ruin of war. In the words of Winston Churchill, he was the 'Organiser of Victory', and no man could wish for a higher accolade than that.

23. Dr John to the Rescue

Four years after the sad death of Emily Roseville, Dr John's services were once again called upon by another member of the family. This time it was Emily's brother, Richard Snowden Andrews, who was in need. 'Snowden' as he was known, had gone South to join the cause, leaving his wife and children in Baltimore. Before the war he had been a successful and prolific architect, with several fine buildings to his credit including the Governor's Residence in Annapolis and the south wing of the U.S. Treasury Building in Washington DC.

Aware that war was imminent, he carefully made scale drawings of Napoleon's cannons, which he smuggled south and used to publish a bestselling book on artillery. In Richmond he formed the First Maryland Artillery, and was soon in the thick of battle.

In August 1862 the Union Army of Virginia, under the command of General John Pope, fell upon Stonewall Jackson's Confederate forces at Cedar Mountain in Culpeper County, Virginia. In the heat of battle, a shell fragment struck Snowden's right side, slicing right through his abdomen to his intestines. The surgeon who attended him took one look and decided there and then there was no hope. As he rode away, Snowden called after him that as a fox-hunting man he had once seen a valuable dog disembowelled over a fence, but he had taken him home to care for him and the dog recovered to hunt again. At this the surgeon relented and called for an ambulance which took him to the nearby farmhouse where he had spent the previous night in the company of Stonewall Jackson. A passing country doctor, Dr Amos, now also looked at the wound and he too shook his head. Snowden replied, *'Isn't there a chance in ten or twenty or even a hundred?'*

Dr John to the Rescue

'*Well,*' replied Dr Amos, '*since you are so plucky, I'll do the best I can for you.*' And with that he cleaned the wound and sewed him up with a needle - but certainly no anaesthetic or disinfectant.

When word of his fate reached his wife in Baltimore, she immediately decided to go to his side, despite having a newborn baby in tow and it being beyond enemy lines. As luck would have it, on her way she met her husband's cousin, my great-grandfather Dr John Contee Fairfax, in Washington. He was very fond of Snowden and agreed to go with her. The journey was not without difficulties and after finally acquiring passports to cross the lines, the little band set off together with a large quantity of brandy supplied by Dr John's friend George W. Riggs, of whom we shall hear more later.

After a long and difficult journey aboard a freight train carrying Union soldiers to the front, they eventually arrived at the farmhouse where Snowden lay. No doubt the sight of his wife and baby proved a great boost to his morale. Dr John did not tarry long, and seeing that his cousin was now in good hands, joined a party of surgeons returning to Washington with the retreating Union Army.

Surprisingly, despite the severity of his wound and the rudimentary care he received, Snowden did not die and when he was finally well enough, he set off to rejoin his comrades in Richmond. Wounded again at the Second Battle of Winchester, he was later appointed an envoy to Germany and lived on until 1903. A silver plate inserted into his abdomen would remain with him for the rest of his life, a souvenir of those grim times.

As for my great-grandfather, we hear no more of him during the remainder of the War, although Constance Burton Harrison reports seeing him in the Confederate capital Richmond, doubtless lending his much needed skills to the care of the countless wounded. We will return to his story when the War is over. In the meantime, we now turn our attention to a member of the Fairfax family who took a different path from all his cousins and very nearly started a war with Great Britain.

24. The Loyalist

If you have got the impression from this story that all the Fairfax's were loyal Sons of Dixie, you would very nearly be right. It is not that they were diehard advocates of slavery or even owned slaves themselves; indeed, as we have heard, the 9th Lord Fairfax and his brother Ferdinando were early pioneers of emancipation. However, they were strong supporters of 'States Rights' - the belief that each state had the right to determine its own policy free from Federal Government interference, although of course slavery did become the central issue. The Fairfax's were Virginians first. They went with their State and thence to the Confederacy it had joined.

However, there was one who did not follow this course and stayed loyal to the Union: Donald McNeill Fairfax. Born at his great-grandfather Bryan Fairfax's old home Mount Eagle in 1818, Donald was the grandson of the luckless Ferdinando Fairfax, who as we have heard in an earlier chapter inherited and then lost an immense fortune from George William Fairfax of Belvoir. Donald's father, Ferdinando's eldest son George William, married Isabella McNeill from New York, the daughter of a prominent US Army engineer, Major General William Gibbs McNeill. Doubtless her influence had much to do with Donald's decision to go with the Union when war came.

Donald joined the US Navy as a midshipman aged 19 and would spend the best part of his life afloat, eventually rising to the rank of Rear-Admiral. It was a hard life but he did well and by 1860 we find Donald serving as a Lieutenant aboard the USS Constellation searching for Southern-bound slave ships off the coast of West Africa. It was on such a patrol that Donald experienced an event so shocking that if he had held any doubts about the evils of slavery, afterwards they would be gone forever. On 25th September they spotted a suspicious vessel making for the high seas. After a brief chase, Lt Fairfax boarded the ship – the Cora - and was horrified to discover a truly hellish scene below the decks. As one of his men would later describe it:

> *'The scene which here presented itself to my eyes baffles description. It was a dreadful sight. They were all packed together like so many sheep: Men, Women, and Children entirely naked, and suffering from hunger and thirst. They had nothing to eat or drink for over 30 hours. As soon as the poor negroes were aware that we were friends to them, they commenced a shouting and yelling like so many wild Indians. They were so overjoyed at being taken by us that I thought they would tear us to pieces.'*

So it is not surprising that when war broke out a year later, Lt Donald Fairfax knew what exactly where his duty lay. He would fight to destroy this great blemish that besmirched the face of America, even if it meant taking the opposite side to his cousins.

25. The Trent Affair

At the very heart of the Southern cause was its faith in the power of 'King Cotton'. In 1860 cotton accounted for 60% of American exports, worth some $200 million a year, so it is not surprising that the cotton producing states believed they ruled the world. It was the ace in their pack. In the words of Senator James Henry Hammond of South Carolina:

> 'Without firing a gun, without drawing a sword, should they make war on us, we could bring the whole world to our feet... What would happen if no cotton was furnished for three years?... England would topple headlong and carry the whole civilized world with her save the South. No, you dare not to make war on cotton. No power on the earth dares to make war upon it. Cotton is King.'

And so it seemed, but as we shall see, events would prove the Senator's words wildly inaccurate.

The Southern states believed that Britain and France would be sure to join them as allies in the coming war, given their heavy dependence on this vital source of supply. To drive the point home, early in 1861 cotton growers throughout the South imposed a pre-emptive ban on exports to Britain and France. The result was that many cotton workers in Lancashire were thrown out of work, causing a great deal of suffering. Their plight was further exacerbated when the Union imposed a blockade of Southern ports, with the result that exports abruptly dropped by 90%. While there is no doubt that this made life very difficult for Britain, cotton stocks in Europe were in fact very high at the time, so cotton consumers were able to ride out the reduction in supply and start sourcing alternatives from India and Egypt.

Perhaps unaware of these facts or simply unwilling to accept them, the Confederate Government was desperate to secure the support of the British and French Governments and after their early victory at Manassas in 1861, they had high hopes of success. Two seasoned politicians, James Murray Mason and John Slidell, were picked for this crucial task. Whatever they had hoped to achieve, they certainly received more than they had bargained for. On their voyage to Europe an incident occurred that caused such a diplomatic furore that it brought Britain to the brink of war with the United States, and in the midst of it was Lt Donald McNeill Fairfax.

This is the story of 'The Trent Affair'.

Evading the Union blockade, Mason and Slidell arrived in Havana early in November. Here they transferred to HMS Trent, a British mail steamer bound for England. The Union was well aware of the envoys' movements and eagerly sought their capture. The USS San Jacinto, under the command of Captain Charles Wilkes, with Lt Donald McNeill Fairfax as second-in-command, was among the ships despatched to track the envoys and seize them should the opportunity arise. By then they were on board a neutral, British ship, safe from Union hands... or so they thought. However, Captain Wilkes had other ideas and when he chanced across the Trent off Cuba, entirely on his own initiative, he decided to strike.

Wilkes was a man known for his fiery temperament: on a previous voyage he had court-martialled his entire company of officers, so he was not one to be defied! Giving the order 'Beat to quarters,' warning shots were fired over the bow of the neutral British ship and eventually she dropped anchor. As the executive officer, it fell to Lt Fairfax to lead the boarding party with orders from Captain Wilkes to seize Mason, Slidell and take the ship as a prize. After some initial resistance, Fairfax arrested the envoys and took them as prisoners back to the San Jacinto. A well-known anecdote is that one of the envoy's wives struck Fairfax across the face with her silk glove, although there is no official record of this.

The Trent Affair

In brave defiance of the fearsome Captain Wilkes, Fairfax had chosen not to seize the ship itself as a prize, for he knew that such an action would almost certainly lead to war with Britain and untold consequences for the Union. This turned out to be a very wise decision for when the news of the envoy's capture became known, all hell broke loose. In the North there were wild celebrations, while in England, predictable outrage.

The British Lion had been insulted and the Lion roared back. The British Prime Minister Lord Palmerston and his Government bristled with righteous indignation, while the public demanded immediate reprisals. At the time, Britain was by far the most powerful country in the world and the Royal Navy really did rule the waves. You simply did not provoke her in this way.

Plans were drawn up to bombard eastern seaports and over 10,000 British troops, including a battalion from the crack Life Guards, were rushed to Canada with the intention of invading Maine. While the two envoys languished in a Northern prison, the diplomatic channels buzzed back and forth between London and Washington. However, bit by bit, the full implications of Captain Wilkes's actions began to sink in and public opinion in the North began to question the wisdom and legality of the envoys' seizure. No doubt the threat of fighting the mighty British Empire, as well as the South, was beginning to have a sobering effect and both sides now began to look in earnest for a way out of this debacle. Eventually, after nearly two months of sabre rattling, a resolution was arrived at, although it was from an unlikely source. As he lay dying from typhoid in December of that year, Queen Victoria's adored husband Prince Albert gave one last service to his adopted country. Summoning up enough strength, he drafted a conciliatory form of words that allowed both the British and the Union to back down with grace. Sure enough by January 1862 the heat had gone out of the affair. The US Government admitted that

Captain Wilkes had acted without official sanction and the British conceded that the Union had really meant no harm to their flag; it had all been an unfortunate misunderstanding! The envoys were duly released into the custody of the British and continued on their way to England.

Perhaps the only person to come out of this sorry affair with his reputation intact was Lt Fairfax. In his official report to the Secretary of the Navy, Gideon Welles, Captain Wilkes wrote:

> *'I cannot close this report without bearing testimony to the admirable manner in which all the officers and men of this ship performed their duties, and the cordial manner in which they carried out my orders. To Lieutenant Fairfax I beg leave to call your particular attention for the praiseworthy manner in which he executed the delicate duties with which he was entrusted; it met and has received my warmest thanks.'*

As for the main protagonists of the Trent Affair, their respective careers would take them in very different directions. The irascible Captain Wilkes soon fell foul of the Navy administration and in 1863 he was court-martialled for insubordination and suspended from duty. Although later pardoned by President Lincoln, he never held command again and retired in 1865. By contrast, Lt Donald Fairfax would go on to command three ships, the Cayuga, Nantucket and Mohawk, and after a distinguished career finally retired in 1881 with the rank of Rear-Admiral.

26. Decline and Fall?

Many years ago, rummaging around one day in the many boxes of papers our grandfather had accumulated during his busy life, I came across a yellowing and battered typed manuscript. Although it had no title, or clue as to its author, as I thumbed my way through the pages, I began to understand that this was the story of the Fairfax family in America, although at the time the characters and places described meant little to me. The people it mentioned were my own kith and kin although at the time the link seemed distant and obscure. Many years would pass before I appreciated the manuscript's significance or that it had been written by my cousin Constance Burton Harrison and read to the New York Historical Society by a Professor Carroll in June 1888.

Although I am familiar with the long and colourful story she revealed in those pages, there was one point that Constance made that seemed at odds with the facts. On the last page Constance concludes with this sad statement:

> *'The Fairfax's in America, who have survived the wreck of health and fortune in that war of ours, are scattered throughout different States. In a graveyard, on the hill between Alexandria and the ruins of Vaucluse, are a group of tombstones bearing the family name. There is little else, today, to tell the passer-by their story in the county called for them.'*

I vividly remember reading those lines and thinking, if only Constance had known what the future held, she might not have written the family off so dolefully.

Writing in 1888, it is easy to understand Constance's feeling of regret for a lost past. The terrible 'War Between the States' had finally ground to a halt in 1865 with the total defeat of the Confederacy, leaving so many of its innumerable victims either dead, crippled, bereaved, orphaned or destitute. The Southern cause never really stood a chance against the industrial might of the North and by the end, those who fought for it would have lost all hope of victory and most hope for the future - their lands had been laid waste and they were broken materially and financially. Only their spirit still flickered on in defiance. 'The South will Rise Again' was their cry, but it would be almost one hundred years before it did and by then no one who lived through its ignominious downfall would be there to see its rebirth.

The Fairfax family, such enthusiastic supporters of the South, had suffered their own share of tragedy. Not only had their home, Vaucluse, 'gone with the wind', but too many had fallen in battle. Among my great-grandfather's cousins, Randolph, the son of Dr Orlando Fairfax, had been killed at the Battle of Fredericksburg in 1862 while Eugene, son of Archibald Blair Fairfax, fell at the Battle of Williamsburg, also that year. Another of Dr Orlando's sons, Ethelbert, was wounded at the Battle of Bentonville in North Carolina in 1865 and Eugene's brother was wounded at the Battle of Seven Pines. Dr Orlando himself was ruined by his loyal investment in Confederate bonds.

However, the outcome was not entirely a disaster for the family. Henry Fairfax, the hero of the Mexican war, had three sons, Raymond, Albert and Herbert. They all survived, as did William Henry, the surgeon son of Wilson Cary Fairfax. True, the family home had gone and although they would never again hold sway in Fairfax County, elsewhere there were signs that not all was lost.

Constance herself fared better than most. Thanks to the foresight of her uncle Reginald Fairfax who, as we saw earlier, invested his fortune in Federal bonds despite serving in the Confederate Navy, Constance and her mother Monimia were able to live in some considerable comfort.

Decline and Fall?

Shortly after the War's end they left for an extended tour of Europe and met a number of well-known literary figures including the celebrated French author Alexander Dumas. On their return to the United States, Constance was reunited with Colonel Burton Harrison. As we learned earlier, he had served as Secretary to President Jefferson Davis and was subsequently imprisoned for two years with other members of the Confederate Government. The love he and Constance had shared in Richmond during the War survived their years of separation and in 1867 they were married, settling in New York. Here these two stalwarts of the Confederacy quickly reinvented themselves. Harrison was called to the New York Bar and practised law successfully for many years, while Constance's reputation as a chronicler of the Old South attracted a wide audience. Many of her works were published in *Scribner's Magazine*, a well-known publication of the time.

By the 1880s they were counted among New York's elite, with a town house on East 29th Street and a rather grand summer 'cottage' at Bar Harbor, Maine, called 'Sea Urchins'. Designed by the well-known architects Rotch & Tilden, with gardens laid out by the fashionable Beatrix Farrand, this ornate seaside residence provided a suitably imposing backdrop where they entertained the glitterati of Bar Harbor's 'Gilded Age' who gathered there every summer. The house still stands today and is occupied by the College of the Atlantic.

Although they are not central to our story, both Constance's sons deserve a brief mention for their considerable achievements. The eldest, Fairfax Harrison, had a distinguished career with the Southern Railroad Company, rising to become President during the First World War and after. Like his mother, he was an enthusiastic amateur historian and published several books during his lifetime. Keenly aware of his Fairfax pedigree, he built a fine country house in Fauquier County, Virginia, which he named 'Belvoir' in tribute to the lost Fairfax mansion on the Potomac.

While Fairfax Harrison was certainly a worthy figure, it was his younger brother Francis Burton Harrison who really stands out: A soldier and then a Congressman, he was appointed Governor-General of the America's most important colony, the Philippines, and was later an advisor to the first presidents of the newly independent country. If his public life was distinguished, his private life was distinguished in an entirely different way: His first wife was Mary Crocker, the grand-daughter of the fabulously rich Californian tycoon Charles Crocker, and after her early death in a motor accident, he would go on to marry a further five times! Along the way he married two sisters in quick succession, Elizabeth and Margaret Wrentmore and lived for several years in Scotland at Teaninich Castle, Easter Ross. Despite his unconventional marital life, he was much admired in the Philippines. He was made an honorary citizen of the country and, at his own request, was buried in Manila.

Let us now return to the main thread of our story as we re-join my great-grandparents in a new chapter of their lives as they set up home and start to raise their family. But before we do, I would like to share a very special day in my life.

Part 5. Beech

27. A Chance Encounter in Rock Creek Cemetery

Over the course of writing this account of our family in America I have often wondered which of my forebears I would most like to have met in person. Some were dynamic, many worthy and others plain eccentric. Perhaps the most colourful and the best company would have been Charlie, the party-loving Californian pioneer. Without the benefit of a time machine we will never meet him, but in May 2012 when I was visiting Virginia and Maryland with my younger brother Rupert, we decided the next best thing would be to pay our respects at his graveside.

Rock Creek Cemetery is one of the oldest in the United States and many a distinguished American lies buried there, among them Charles Snowden Fairfax and his devoted wife Ada. Driving through the gates we were overwhelmed by the immense number of graves that stretched into the distance. How on earth would we ever find those of Charlie and Ada? We had a packed schedule and realised it might take us hours to find them. Then, as if by Divine Providence, an elderly man pulled up alongside us and asked in his rich Southern drawl, *'Can I help you gentlemen?'* There was something in his manner that was gracious, kind and benevolent all at the same time. Had he been sent to guide us? Gratefully accepting his offer of directions and a map we set off on our search. Not long after Rupert called out, *'I've found them and they're not alone!'* They certainly were not alone.

For alongside Charlie and Ada, what we found was the last resting place of our great-grandfather and his entire family. Lying head to head, there were the graves of our great-grandparents, Dr John Contee Fairfax and his wife

Mary Kirby, his mother, Caroline Snowden Fairfax, and all their children and wives. These were our great aunts and uncles: Caroline, Josephine, Mary, Charles Edmund, his wife Lillian, Frances and her two husbands, Edward Lowndes Rhett and Clarence Roberts. Albert, who emigrated to England and is buried in Yorkshire, is not forgotten here either: a small plaque to his memory stands among the graves.

Standing in the warm spring sunshine before the graves, we imagined all the times they must have shared, both good and bad and the love they had for one another. To see them lying there together, as if peacefully asleep in a giant bed, was entirely unexpected and very moving. Then slowly the thought dawned on us: these were not just Charlie's family, they were our family – our own flesh and blood - our long-lost American family.

Strolling back to our car, we could hear the sound of singing coming from St Paul's Church, which stands in the middle of the graveyard, and as it was a Sunday, we decided to go in. To our great surprise this was not just a regular Sunday service - we had stumbled upon the celebration of the Church's 300th Anniversary, presided over by no less than three Bishops in full regalia, accompanied by the beautiful spirituals of the Washington Boys Choir!

Of all the days we could have picked to visit out forebears' graves, we had picked that one. The coincidence was almost too remarkable to believe. It was as if we had been led there - perhaps we had? As we drove out through the gates, the same elderly black gentleman pulled up beside us. '*I hope you found what you were looking for?*' he asked in his soft drawl. '*Yes*,' we replied. We certainly had - and more.

So let us now return to Dr John, his wife Mary, and the place they called home: Northampton.

28. Northampton

At the beginning of 1865, just as the war came to its unhappy ending, Dr John Fairfax and his wife Mary decided the time had come to find a home of their own. Until then they had lived at Woodburn, Sandy Spring, the home of Dr John's mother Caroline and her second husband Colonel Sanders. Their first born, Caroline, had arrived in 1858 and now with another on the way, whom they would christen Josephine, the need for more space had become imperative.

So in March of that year, a few short weeks before Robert E. Lee surrendered his starving and woebegone Confederate Army to Ulysses S. Grant at Appomattox Court House, my great-grandparents purchased an old plantation near Largo in Prince George's County, Maryland. Known as Northampton, it would remain in the Fairfax family until my parents finally sold it in 1959, shortly after my birth.

Northampton was a famous old plantation that had been in the Sprigg family since 1673, when 1,000 acres were granted to Thomas Sprigg. Many generations of that family lived there until 1865 when it was sold to Dr John and his wife.

The Sprigg family were well known in Maryland and several had distinguished themselves in national and local life. First among them was Osborn Sprigg Jr, a prominent local member of the Provincial Convention in Annapolis during the Revolutionary period, and responsible for creating the fine house that Dr John acquired. In a survey of 1798 the house was described as being 60 by 40 feet with a hip roof and valued at $850, a large sum for the time. In addition, there was a 36 by 26 ft kitchen building, a 36 by 26 ft wash house, a 16 ft square meat house, a 12 ft square milk house, and other sundry farm buildings. Not far from the house was a large lake, surrounded by formal gardens that had been laid out by the celebrated designer of Washington DC, Pierre L'Enfant.

Upon Osborn's death in 1815 the property passed to his nephew Samuel, who in 1819 became Governor of Maryland. Samuel was an enthusiastic supporter of the scheme to build the Chesapeake and Ohio Canal and later served as the canal company's president. Following his death in 1855, his widow Violetta lived on at Northampton until 1865 when she finally sold it to my great-grandparents.

It was not a modest dwelling and the very fact that Dr John was able to consider buying it tells us something of his situation at the end of the war. As a Marylander, he had survived the traumas of the conflict rather better than some of his cousins in Virginia and he was clearly not short of funds at this time, as has sometimes been thought - his problems would come later. However, Northampton, with its 713 acres of good quality tobacco farmland, was probably more than he could afford on his own. In any case, he was a doctor and his knowledge of farming was almost certainly very limited. Casting around for a solution, Dr John sought out his old friend George W. Riggs, whom we met earlier during the frantic mission of mercy to save his badly injured cousin Richard Snowden Andrews in 1862. Riggs, a successful merchant in Washington and the founder of Riggs & Co, later known as Riggs National Bank, was in a position to help. He had recently bought a property nearby at Chillum, called Green Hill, formerly the home of the Degges family, so may have seen this as a logical way to expand his farming interests, while at the same time helping out his old friend. Whatever the reason, they pooled their resources and together they bought Northampton as partners.

Life at Northampton must have been idyllic for the young Fairfax family and soon two more daughters arrived, Caroline and Josephine. Shortly after the death of Dr John's elder brother Charles Snowden Fairfax early in 1869, a little boy was born. His parents named him Charlie, doubtless in memory of his recently departed uncle, but tragically his life would be all too brief, for he passed away within the year, an all too frequent occurrence in those days. Happily, Mary was already expecting another child and a month after little Charlie's death, on 23rd June 1870, another son was born.

They named him Albert after his grandfather and Kirby after his mother's family. He had curly red hair, perhaps a throwback to his distant Viking ancestry, and for that reason he was always known as Beech, after the copper beech tree, so that is what we shall call him from now on. One day in the future and a long way from Maryland, he too would marry and his eldest son would be our father.

As I write this story in the early 21st century, it seems incredible to me that our grandfather was born so long ago and in such a different age. To put it in perspective, our grandfather was born five years after the end of the Civil War and six years before Custer's Last Stand at the Battle of the Little Big Horn! By a happy stroke of luck, his birth also coincided with a pivotal moment in American history: the old order had been swept away by the Civil War and an exciting new age was beginning that would see America take the lead from the old European countries as the economic powerhouse of the world. Huge changes would occur and immense wealth would be generated. Beech would play his part in all this and in time would set the Fairfax family on a very different path from the life his American forebears had enjoyed since they settled in the New World so many generations before.

That is jumping ahead. Let us return to the bucolic life of Dr John and his wife Mary at their fine old Maryland property, Northampton. Soon, other children followed Beech: Mary was born in 1871, then in 1876 a brother, Charles, Edmund (always referred to by his second name) and finally Frances in 1878, twenty years after her eldest sister Caroline!

Like many young couples before and since, it was not long before they set about making improvements to their new home, adding such features as the dormer windows elegantly adorned with 'Gothic Revival' verge-boards. They also turned their attention to the gardens and from an article published in the Baltimore Sun newspaper many years later we get a vivid impression of the magical world they created:

> *'The house, some 200 years old, is of frame, about 125 feet front and such portion as is the original architecture is put together without nails (i.e. with pegs). The drawing room, library and dining room, all with high chimney pieces and wide open fireplaces, face the front and in the rear, according to the fashion of that time, are bedrooms with high Gothic windows and other rooms now used as pantries. The place is well wooded and about the residence are elm and willow trees, also flowering magnolia trees and white fringe trees trailing their delicate blossoms. There is a real lover's walk winding between a hedge of old-fashioned lilacs that bend in clusters of purple and white fragrance through the early spring sunshine. Quaint yellow daffodils scatter their gold amid April's grasses and June unfolds the warmth of color and incense of myriad hundred leaved roses. There are stately poplar trees also and in a grove is a well of olden days with a well house built over it.'*

The article goes on to describe *'relics of the negro quarters of plantation days,'* a polite way of describing the former slave quarters, which today are preserved as a museum. One very old former slave called Uncle Robert still lived there together with his children and grandchildren and when the article was written in 1905 he was reckoned to be 100 years old. This fine old gentleman was clearly held in great esteem and when Frances, the youngest member of the family married in 1903, Uncle Robert 'viewed the picturesque open-air wedding from a chair of state upon the veranda and felt the importance of his duties in speeding the bride in the old family coach upon her wedding journey.'

Although details of life at Northampton in those days are sketchy, one can well imagine the carefree existence these children would have enjoyed roaming their extensive acreage and playing with friends and cousins who came to call. Through his mother's family the Snowdens, Dr John was connected to the most prominent families in the county and they would all visit one another regularly.

A frequent visitor to Northampton was their young cousin Emily Rosalie Marshall, whose mother Emily Roseville had died after giving birth at the Fairfax's former home, Woodburn. (The late Giles Mills, whose knowledge of our shared history in those times has been invaluable, was her grandson.) The same age as Dr John's eldest daughter Caroline, a favourite family story tells of how the two little girls had one day crept into the still-room, where they found a large bowl of cherries in brandy. They tasted it and liking what they found, tasted it some more until they were eventually found insensible on the floor. I might add that the young ladies were just four years old at the time!

But Northampton was not just a place of rural beauty and entertainment, for its chief purpose was to raise the crop for which Prince George's County was famous: tobacco. Maryland had been a slave owning state and before the Civil War, the economy had boomed on the back of the 'peculiar institution', as it was politely called. Now with its abolition, plantation owners had to change their ways to survive. Some did but many others gave up and their plantations were sold off. Northampton was no exception and its purchase from the Sprigg family by Dr John Fairfax in 1865 was part of this process, marking a turning point in its history. No longer would the fields be worked by slaves but by free men.

The immediate effect of this was a dramatic collapse in agricultural production. Whereas in 1860 Prince George's County produced a staggering 13 million tons of tobacco, by 1870 this had fallen to less than 4 million. The same went for other agricultural products and Prince George's County, once so prosperous, was now reduced to poverty. Over the next thirty years, as more people settled here and the number of small farms increased, a measure of prosperity would return, but the elegant lifestyle its fortunate white plantation owners had once enjoyed was to be gone forever.

29. The Grit in the Oyster

While the largely agrarian Southern economy stagnated, the picture was very different in the more industrialised North. The War's aftermath had brought a sudden and dramatic resurgence in economic activity, most clearly demonstrated by a boom in railroad building. Driven by land grants and Government subsidies, between 1868 and 1873 over 33,000 miles of track were laid and the rail industry became the country's largest employer after agriculture. The peak of this boom was the completion of the Transcontinental Railroad linking the east and west coasts, with the driving of the 'Golden Spike' at Promontory Summit, Utah, on 10th May 1869.

It goes without saying that the boom attracted speculators from all corners of the earth, and among them was George W. Riggs, Dr John's partner in Northampton. It was a classic asset bubble and for a while everyone thought they had struck it rich. Then in 1873 an event occurred that would have far-reaching consequences for the inhabitants of Northampton and, strangely enough, not least for the little three year-old boy who would become our grandfather, Albert Kirby Fairfax.

It all started in Europe, when a seizure in the banking system caused a sudden collapse in asset prices around the world. This came to be known as the Panic of 1873 and would lead to the Long Depression which lasted until 1879. During this period over 18,000 businesses, including many banks, went bust.

George W. Riggs and his bank survived the Long Depression, but at a price. It was a hammer blow to the struggling farming business at Northampton and by 1881 we find Riggs and Fairfax facing ruin. The farm had obviously been running at a loss for many years and its debt had been mounting to worrying levels. Unable to fund this themselves, they turned to Dr John's mother, Caroline Sanders, who lived with them at Northampton and, as will become apparent, was the person who held the purse strings. From her first husband Albert Fairfax, Dr John's father, she would have inherited a substantial share of Thomas 9th Lord Fairfax's fortune. Perhaps her second husband Colonel Sanders had also provided for her. So in April that year, we find Riggs and Fairfax mortgaging Northampton to Caroline Sanders to secure payment of their debt.

This was no answer to their problems and within a year they had defaulted on the mortgage. This was a real tragedy and put Caroline in a very difficult position. On the one hand, Northampton was the family home and the security of her family and grandchildren was at stake. Perhaps she could have forgiven her son and his partner their default or carried the sum forward? On the other hand, there was obviously no sense in throwing good money after bad. So, doubtless with a heavy heart and to the despair of the whole family, Caroline felt obliged to put Northampton up for sale at auction in June 1882.

The day that everyone in the family had dreaded finally arrived and no doubt a great crowd gathered for the auction - Northampton was a famous old house and the Fairfax's were considered among the elite of Prince George's County. How utterly humiliating the whole affair must have been for this once great family, brought low by debt.

However, I am happy to tell you this was not the end of the road for the family at Northampton for in an extraordinary turn of events, at the last moment Caroline weakened and herself bought the property for $20,000!

With this remarkable *volte-face* Caroline became the sole proprietor of Northampton and would remain so until her death in 1899 at the great age of 91. Whether this was just a sudden change of heart or something she had planned, we can only guess. Whatever the truth, the family was now able to continue living there and it would remain in their ownership right up into this author's lifetime. Dr John finally inherited Northampton after his mother's death in 1899 but he outlived her for only one year and when he died in 1900, ownership of the farm then passed to Beech, although he would never live there in his adult life.

The bare facts of this episode are strange enough but they only hint at the human side to the story. It goes without saying that this must have been a desperately traumatic time for the family and the cause of a great deal of anxiety. Northampton was their business and their home, and the threatened loss of security would have affected everyone. One can only imagine the long drawn out arguments and counter arguments that would have taken place over these months.

For Beech these events could not have come at a more impressionable age. Now aged twelve, a difficult time for most children, the prospect of losing Northampton must have been terribly humiliating. After all, he would have been raised on tales of the family's glorious times in England and Virginia: how the brave Sir Thomas defeated the King in the English Civil War and the family's golden days in Colonial times when they rode to hounds with their friend the great George Washington. What's more, wasn't the head of the family entitled to call himself 'Lord' Fairfax, a great honour accorded to few men? Why had they turned their back on all this and how had they managed to become so reduced in the world?

Perhaps this was the moment that lit the fire in his belly and set him on the course to ensure the family would never again suffer such ignominy. Maybe one day he too would reclaim the family's title and take his rightful place in the House of Lords? What a thrilling dream for a young boy born and raised in rural Maryland – but maybe it was more than just a fantasy, perhaps he really could do it?

Whatever the case, Beech now realised that life could not go on in its sleepy way. Things would have to change and even if it meant leaving the idyllic surroundings of Northampton, he became determined to rebuild the family's fortune and reclaim the title so long ignored. It was the very grit in his oyster.

30. The Long Road

Beech's plan to rebuild the family fortune and position in the world was never going to be easy. The crisis had left the family bereft and life must have been decidedly precarious. Unlike his father there would be no university education for Beech, no assumption of a position in the world. If he was going to make it, it would have to be by his own sweat, toil and determination.

Of course life is never as clear-cut as history sometimes likes to make out. Motives and actions that seem obvious from a distance are never that clear at the time. Certainly, there was no future on the farm in Maryland but any grand ambitions would probably have developed slowly in his head. So early in 1888 he bade farewell to his family and took the train to New York where he found a job as a trainee bank clerk with Brown Brothers, the respected Wall Street firm that had been established in 1818. The original business, Alex Brown, was first established in Baltimore, close to the family home, so perhaps there was already a contact in New York that helped him on his way.

However, this was no cushy internship. It was more like a baptism of fire.

Perhaps the best description of his early career comes from Beech himself. By chance, the text of a speech he made at a boys' school in London in 1926 has survived. His heartfelt words tell of a lifetime of struggle and yearning for a childhood so abruptly curtailed. There is no empty rhetoric in his encouragement to the boys to follow his example and rise up to meet the challenges that they would face. This came from the heart, born out of hard experience and is strikingly frank:

> *'Unfortunately, I have only enjoyed such privileges that are offered here to a very slight degree, as my school days only*

lasted three years, and then I had to go out into the world to a larger and more exacting curriculum...At the age of 18 I left my own home on the farm in Maryland, never to return again as a resident, although I still own it, and have an affectionate remembrance of my boyhood days there.

When I left I was given by my father £5, or $25, and my fare to New York, and there I obtained a job in a bank at $5, or £1, a week.

As it was January the weather was very cold, so out of my £5 I purchased an overcoat for £3 or $15, but shortly after reaching New York I was persuaded to become an usher at a Church in New York, which I used to do on Sundays, and one evening while assisting at the Mission of the Church some unkind friend stole my coat, so I had to go through the winter without a topcoat, as my salary scarcely permitted the wherewithal to exist let alone another coat, and Winters in New York are far more drastic than in England.

Please forgive this story, but it teaches a lesson.

I venture to think that all of the boys here are very fortunate in being able to enjoy such privileges as are offered by the Grove House School.

My experience is that boys seldom realise such opportunities as these until it is too late. I know I did not to my sorrow for I have had to fight all my life and make opportunities, and I feel that no matter how blue things may seem we should never be downhearted or lose faith, but should always rise above adversity, which we can always do if you are sufficiently determined...

You must persevere and be obedient to your superiors and teachers and, at all times, retain your self-respect, and then you will be respected by others.

The Long Road

As certain as day follows night, if you adhere to such tenets you will carve out successful careers.'

Without knowing how Beech's remarkable life would turn out, you might well be surprised to find him making a speech as Lord Fairfax, guest of honour at a school in London. After all, he was born and raised an American and this story has up to now been about those doughty citizens of the Republic, the Fairfax family of America?

The truth is that by 1926 he had been a naturalised Englishman for nearly twenty years, having successfully proved his claim to the family's ancient title in 1908, and was now able to sit in the House of Lords. He was a pillar of the British establishment, successful and prosperous. He was the owner of his own discount house in the City of London, married to our grandmother with two sons, our father and uncle, and with two splendid homes at his disposal, one in a fashionable part of London and another in the country. Quite an achievement for the young man who had left the family farm in Maryland aged 18 with only $25 in his pocket!

The question is, how did he achieve all this in less than the forty years since the day he caught the train to New York and, more to the point, why did he turn his back on the exciting 'New World' that so many generations of the Fairfax family had called home, in favour of the 'Old Country'? How very strange when the world seemed to be going in the opposite direction!

For us, his British descendants, this is the heart of the story. It is odd to think that had he not taken this path, we would be American citizens and England merely a quaint place to visit 'on vacation', rather than our home.

To begin to find the answer to these questions we must now go back to those early days in New York and catch up with the humble bank clerk from Maryland as he sets out on the long road to success.

31. New York

One can only wonder at the shock the eighteen year old Beech must have felt that day as he stepped down from the train into the steaming melting pot that was the New York of the late 1880s. The contrast between his boyhood in rural Maryland and his new life in the seething metropolis is hard to imagine.

For New York really was a melting pot. By 1890, close to half its population of one and a half million were immigrants from Europe: Italians, Irish, British, Germans, Scandinavians, East Europeans swelled its numbers, packed into squalid tenements, speaking a babble of foreign tongues. Crime and corruption, vice and violence were the city's constant themes, while in sharp contrast, on the Upper East side, the rich lived out a gilded existence in their elegant mansions. Everywhere people were hurrying, racing to survive, racing to get rich and everywhere new buildings were going up. The Pulitzer Building on Park Row was one of the first and it would be followed by many more marvels, such as the famous Flatiron Building early in the new century.

Just how Beech fitted in to this frenzied world we can only guess. However, for now his only concern was survival and the $25 he was given by his father was not going to last long. What Beech lacked in financial resources he made up in strength of character and a steely determination not to fail. The job he landed at Brown Brothers was far from glamorous, indeed it must have been extremely humdrum and repetitive, but it did teach him to value good book keeping and this was something he would practice throughout his life. As a man who started with nothing to his name, every cent that came his way was accounted for throughout his life, and in the large archive he left behind there are numerous accounting books recording every one of those cents.

Day to day life was a struggle for the young Beech. Several stories have come down to us in the family that illustrate this: how the irreplaceable overcoat he purchased with his scant resources was stolen; how his lunch consisted of a single apple and how he resorted to selling hot chestnuts on the street corner to help make ends meet. I hope his life was not just unremitting hardship, after all many people have to struggle when young and still manage to enjoy themselves. Perhaps he did what many a young New Yorker did - attended baseball matches, or went to dance halls? Perhaps there were young ladies in his life, but if there were he kept them very quiet.

I would also like to think that his cousin Constance Burton Harrison, the celebrated writer who also lived in New York, took him under her wing. After all she and her husband were by now well-established figures in New York society and as the great chronicler of the Fairfax family, I think we can safely assume she did much to fire up Beech's interest in its history. Her essays on the family's golden days in Virginia appeared regularly in Scribner's Magazine and doubtless he would have dwelled on these stories as he slogged away on his clerk's stool, dreaming perhaps that one day he would restore the family to its former prominent position.

As well as learning the rudiments of banking, Beech also made some useful friends in those days and none more so than a young Englishman called Montagu Norman, who would later rise to the zenith of the British establishment as Governor of the Bank of England. Almost exactly the same age as Beech, Norman had been sent to New York to gain experience at Brown Brothers, but in sharp contrast to his young American friend, Norman had enjoyed every advantage. Educated at Eton College and Cambridge

University, Norman's father was a partner of Martin's Bank and his maternal grandfather, Sir Mark Collet, was Governor of the Bank of England in the 1880s. So this was an unlikely friendship, Beech the inky clerk and Norman pre-destined for the boardroom.

However, the two did become friends. After Beech's death in 1939, it fell to my grandmother to deal with the winding up of the Discount House he would later found. A long correspondence between her and the Governor of the Bank of England ensued, among which are some interesting clues to this unlikely friendship. In one letter she says that as he lay dying, '*He often spoke to me of the time you and he were together in New York.*' Norman obviously admired Beech and in another letter says that his success was built '*largely on the strength of your husband's character and force.*' As we shall see later, this early friendship would play a vital role in the development of Beech's business career in London.

Norman, blessed with an air of confidence often found among those born with a strong sense of entitlement, doubtless made quite an impression on the young Beech. Equally Norman must have been fascinated to discover that this young American bank clerk might one day be entitled to call himself Lord Fairfax. After all, in those days, a peerage was taken very seriously and Beech's father Dr John Contee held the unique, albeit unacknowledged, position as 'The only Peer Resident in America'. Perhaps it was Norman's early influence that awoke in Beech a curiosity about the 'Old Country'. After all, one can quite easily see that Britain, then at the peak of its Imperial power, appeared an altogether more attractive and civilised place than the brash world he inhabited. Maybe one day he would claim his rightful place in the House of Lords, and play his part in that refined and elegant world? For now, it would have to remain a dream.

However, Beech was no dreamer - nothing could be further from the truth. He was a hard-headed pragmatist who realised the only way to achieve his goals was through sheer hard work. But he was certainly ambitious and in his quiet way determined to restore the family to its former position in the world.

Over ten years rolled by and slowly he rose up through the ranks, although the likelihood of rebuilding the family fortune must have seemed impossibly remote in those days. Bank clerks usually remained bank clerks throughout their lives, even those with ancient titles, and opportunities to climb the ladder were few and far between, or so it seemed. Then, as the new century dawned, a series of events conspired to change all that and propel Beech in a direction no one, least of all him, might have expected.

32. The New Century: A Break with the Past

Autumn 1899, just as the leaves were beginning to turn and the old century slowly drew to its close, Beech's 91-year-old grandmother, Caroline Snowden Sanders, finally passed away. How extraordinary to think that she was born less than a decade after George Washington's death. Her first husband Albert Fairfax had died in 1835 aged only 33, while Caroline remarried and went on to live throughout almost the whole of the 19th century, witnessing America grow from a frontier country into the emerging powerhouse of the world. As the senior member of the family for so long, it was Caroline who ruled the roost and held the purse strings. Her influence on the family had been strong yet benign and her death marked the end of an era, coming as it did so near the end of the old century. When Beech's father, the good old Dr John also died, just a year later in 1900, the break with the past was complete. Ownership of Northampton now passed to Beech, although he would never live there himself and it fell to his mother and then his sister Frances to manage the property in his absence.

By this time, most of the family had flown the nest that had been Northampton. Beech's second eldest sister Josephine had married Tunstall Smith in 1892 and now lived in Baltimore with their two daughters, Josephine and Louise. His eldest sister Caroline, who never married, also lived in Baltimore, while several other members of the family had followed Beech's example and moved to New York. From the 1900 Census records we can see that Beech, Edmund, Mary (usually known by her second name Cecilia) all lived at 105 East 45th Street together with their cousin Minna Kirby. Only the youngest, Frances, still remained at Northampton with her widowed mother, Mary Kirby, who would live on until 1912.

Dr John had been well regarded in Maryland as a modest, scholarly man and had no particular interest in his title, other than as a quaint historical curiosity. The family were American and had been for many generations, so the idea of appending a title to his name must have seemed entirely archaic, not to say ridiculous. During his lifetime, the family had kept almost completely out of the limelight, save for the odd newspaper article telling of the family's glorious past. That aside, there was really nothing to add. However, with Dr John's death all that was about to change.

By the turn of the century, in contrast to the attitudes of their forebears, Americans had become infatuated with the romance of British titles. For the nouveaux riches of America, there was nothing more exciting than to have your daughter marry an English lord, earl or, best of all, a duke! For Americans, a title in the family brought respectability and glamour, with the opportunity to meet the Royal Family. For the struggling British aristocracy, weighed down with crumbling estates and the desire to keep up appearances, the enormous dowries these young American ladies brought with them were often the only hope of staving-off ruin. So many of these young heiresses made the voyage to England that the author Frances Hodgson Burnett even coined a term for it: 'The Shuttle'. Among the more famous were Consuelo Vanderbilt, who married the Duke of Marlborough, and Jennie Jerome, who married the Duke's brother, Lord Randolph Churchill and produced Britain's greatest ever Prime Minister, Winston Churchill.

In this atmosphere of intense 'Anglomania' the discovery by the American press that a young man eligible to call himself Lord Fairfax was living in their midst was fascinating. So, with his father's death Beech was unwittingly thrust into the public eye and suddenly the papers were full of headlines proclaiming 'Lord Fairfax A Clerk In Wall Street Office' and 'British Lord Is Working As A Clerk'.

The New Century: A Break with the Past

Luckily for us, Beech was an assiduous collector and among the many artefacts that have come down to us is a fascinating scrap-book. Although battered and bent on the outside, inside there is real gold: pasted to the cardboard pages is article after article telling us of Beech's new life as a celebrity. Of course, he was a rather strange fish – titled yet unentitled, and an American of many generations standing. What their readers made of him is hard to say - after all, he was certainly not glamorous and went out of his way to remind journalists that he was a simple bank clerk. A more unlikely celebrity could not be imagined and he hardly played up to his new fame. However, to the American press the very fact that he was 'Lord Fairfax' was enough to make him newsworthy.

This flurry of excitement would probably have subsided and the press moved on to more exciting titbits had Queen Victoria not died the very next year. She had reigned over the British Empire, the greatest the world had ever seen, for more than 63 years and would now be succeeded by her eldest son, the pleasure loving Edward VII, affectionately known as 'Tum-Tum' for obvious reasons. The Coronation was scheduled for 1902 and all Peers of the Realm were summoned to attend.

Despite the family's long-standing lack of interest in the title and their strongly held loyalty to the United States, the death of Dr John Contee Fairfax, 11th Lord Fairfax, had not gone unnoticed in London. Succession to a peerage is automatic, whoever and wherever the new Peer of the Realm may be, even if he is a member of a family that had been American long before Independence. So what a surprise it must have been for Beech when an enveloped heavily embossed with the seal of the 'Lord Great Chamberlain's Office' dropped through the letterbox one fine morning bearing the invitation to the King's Coronation!

This was an extraordinary turn of events: the very thought of travelling to London to attend this great state occasion, surrounded by the crowned heads of Europe and the massed ranks of the British aristocracy resplendent in ermine and robes, their heads crowned with coronets, must have seemed incredible to Beech. However, swallowing whatever doubts he might have had, he duly accepted.

Not unnaturally, with this the press went wild and suddenly the papers were full of headlines such as '*Edward VII Invites One Yankee to His Coronation*' and '*The Only American to be Commanded to King Edward's Coronation*'. Some went even further: '*New Yorker Claims Title to English Barony*', '*New Yorker's Right to Scotch Peerage*' and '*Mr Fairfax Wants a Title*'. Now Beech was at the centre of everyone's attention and there was nothing this shy, modest man could do to get away from it.

As things turned out, Beech never did go to the Coronation. The King developed appendicitis, then a life-threatening condition, and so the ceremony, scheduled for 24th June, was postponed until 9th August. Unfortunately for Beech, the news arrived too late as he had already set sail from New York. This must have been a great blow - after all, crossing the Atlantic was not something one did on a whim, quite apart from the cost. However, there was nothing to be done: titled or not, bank clerks could not enjoy two-month sojourns abroad as the leisured classes might, so after only a few days in England and a brief visit to York, the ancient home of the family, he packed his bags and returned to New York.

It was always said that this first visit to England did not impress him much and this seems likely as it turned out very differently to what he had planned. However, the journey was by no means a waste of time and the fact that he had been acknowledged as a member of the Peerage in England, worthy of an invitation to the King Emperor's coronation, would, as we shall later see, open doors to a life Beech could only have dreamed of up to then.

33. Romance in the Air!

The new century was certainly proving to be full of promise and bright new opportunities, but it was not only Beech who was attracting attention. For other members of the family too, things were also looking up. So before we hear more about the exciting developments that would sweep Beech onwards towards a new life, let us briefly catch up with their lives.

The new century began in splendid fashion with the marriage of Beech's cousin, Francis, the younger son of Constance Burton Harrison, to the San Francisco born heiress Mary Crocker. The bride was quite a catch, being the heiress to the Crocker railroad and banking fortune and the wedding at Tuxedo Park was a lavish affair widely reported in the press. How Constance's heart must have swelled with pride!

We get a very good description of this high society occasion from a report in the *New York Herald* dated 8th June 1900. A special train of 'drawing room cars' was charted to convey the guests from Jersey City to Tuxedo Park for the ceremony at St Mary's Church. As the Hamptons are today, so Tuxedo Park was then the favoured retreat for the rich and famous. Adele Colgate, George Fisher Baker, J.P. Morgan, William Waldorf Astor and Herbert C. Pell were just some of the grandees counted among its residents.

As one might expect, no expense was spared: *'the church was festooned with garlands of laurel and sweet smelling cedar, and on the posts of the pews were clusters of white roses and syringias. Just at the arch of the chancel was suspended a wedding bell of white roses, and tall palms on either side of the altar formed a graceful arch over the heads if the bridal party.'*

The report goes on to tell us that the bridesmaids were dressed, *'in graceful gowns of white mousseline de soie, with insertions of Cluny lace over white taffeta and sashes of pink crepe de Chine that fell to the edge of the skirts...their hats of yellow straw were trimmed with pink flowers. All carried shower bouquets of pink sweet peas.'*

As befitting an heiress, the bride's wedding dress itself was a sight to behold: *'Her gown was a beautiful creation...it was elegant but severely plain of ivory white satin, with long square train, the square cut bodice being filled in with Brussels point lace. The veil was an exquisite confection of Brussels point, that fell from the head to the very end of the long train, the effect being that of a costume being made entirely of lace...the bridal bouquet was of white orchids, with delicate hints of mauve, fringed with natural orange blossoms. The only jewel the bride wore was a pear shaped pearl pendant of delicate rose color, set in a tiny spray of diamonds, the bridegroom's gift. This was attached to a slender gold chain, set in diamonds.'*

The ushers included Archibald Harrison, brother of the bride, Beech, his cousin the novelist Gouverneur Morris, Frederick d'Hauteville, William Sloane and Benjamin Cable. After the service, the party moved onto the wedding breakfast at the home of Mrs Charles B. Alexander, where they dined on a grand feast of *'Oeufs Brouilles aux Truffes, Saumon Froid sauce Ravigote, Filet de Boeuf aux Champignons, Haricots Vertes, Pouissins Grilles, and Pointes D'Aspereges a L'Huile'*, followed by ice cream, raspberries and chocolates, all washed down with Champagne!

One wonders if the Harrison family felt a little overwhelmed by this conspicuous display of new wealth, and as if to make the point that they came from an old aristocratic Southern family, the loving cup was drunk from a magnificent Cary family silver vessel dated 1772.

Sadly the marriage was destined to be short lived. Supported by his wife's wealth, Francis was elected to Congress in 1902 and their future looked very promising. Then tragedy struck, when in November 1905 Mary was killed in a motor accident on Long Island, leaving two young daughters.

In contrast with this sumptuous display of wealth and glitz that united new money with old breeding, the next family wedding was an altogether more traditional affair, when in October 1903 Beech's youngest sister Frances married the son of an old and distinguished family from South Carolina, Edward Lowndes Rhett. The groom, a stockbroker in New York, was described in various newspaper reports as 'well known in the Four Hundred' (a term used to describe the social elite of New York, supposedly derived from the number who could fit comfortably into Mrs Astor's ballroom), and a member of various clubs including the Knickerbocker, the Calumet, Crescent Athletic and Union League clubs. Obviously a man of impeccable respectability and a perfect match for the well-born and beautiful Miss Fairfax.

The *Baltimore Sun* newspaper gives us a charming description of the wedding at the old Fairfax property:

> *'The romance and picturesqueness of the Colonial days in Maryland seemed to have returned yesterday in Prince George's County when Miss Frances Marvin Fairfax daughter of Lady Fairfax and the late Lord Fairfax and sister of Lord Fairfax, Baron Cameron was married to Mr Edward Lowndes Rhett of New York City...at Northampton, the Colonial residence once the home to Governor Sprigg.*
>
> *The broad staircase was twined with English Ivy and white chrysanthemums and clusters of the same tall flowers wreathed the Colonial doorways. In the drawing room a royal fire of hickory logs burned upon the hearth, its color reproduced in autumnal foliage and white roses upon the walls and about the chimneypiece. In the library across the hall a similar fire lit up the portraits of lords and ladies of yore...*
>
> *The bridal procession passed down the quaint stairway and between ribbon aisles to a shrine of evergreens and*

white roses beneath a century-old willow tree. Not the least artistic feature of the charming picture was the 30 or more black family servants, who formed a colourful background to the scene. The place of honour was accorded to Uncle Robert, now over 100 years old, but once coachman to Governor Sprigg.

The bride wore a dainty gown of white crepe de chine over white silk, with tulle veil caught with orange blossoms, and carried lilies of the valley. She was attended by her sister, Miss Cecilia Fairfax, who wore a costume of white etamine, combined with lace and chiffon, and a white picture hat with ostrich plumes, and carried a cluster of bridesmaid roses. The tiny flower girls were Misses Josephine and Louise Tunstall Smith, (nieces of the bride) who wore frocks of white mousseline and lace, and carried bridesmaid roses.'

Guests came from far and wide, and of course most of the old Maryland families were represented such as the Bowies, Berrys, Carys, Carters, Kirbys, and Roberts. But there was one person missing, the one who really should have been there - Beech. As we shall see, he was far away in London, embarking on an exciting new chapter in his life, but how sad that for him and his family that this meant missing such an important and happy occasion.

34. The Big Break

As the great tycoon Andrew Carnegie famously put it: 'The rising man must do something exceptional, and beyond the range of his special department. HE MUST ATTRACT ATTENTION.' Quite unintentionally, Beech, our rising man, had done just that and the next few years would see him rapidly rise from lowly bank clerk to the commanding heights of a partnership at a Wall Street brokerage house.

Carnegie's dictum was certainly right and no one could have missed the volumes of press attention devoted to the bank clerk-cum-lord; none more so than the directors of a recently formed bank, The International Banking Corporation.

This new bank had the backing of several well-known American financiers, including Alfred G. Vanderbilt, H.C. Frick, Edwin Gould (son of Jay Gould), and William Salomon. It had been set up to deal in letters of credit and bills of exchange - in other words, international trade finance. Casting around for someone to help run the London branch, the directors alighted upon Beech as the ideal candidate.

In July 1902, shortly after his return from the abortive coronation trip, he was offered the job of sub-manager in their London branch and by October, although he had missed the coronation, he was back in England once again.

This was Beech's Big Break: all those years of hard work were finally paying off, but of course that was not the only reason they chose him. It was the title, of course, and the access they assumed it would bring.

As ever the papers were quick off the mark to report Beech's departure for London and many assumed it would be forever. But within two years he was back in New York, as one newspaper explained: 'Lord Fairfax's Mission to Great Britain A Failure'. The blame was not Beech's, but had more to do with a reluctance of British capitalists to invest overseas. The hope that Beech's title would open the right doors seems also to have been misguided. There had been several scandals in recent years involving members of the aristocracy, who unwittingly lent their names to shady operations, and these had left investors with a distinct aversion to anything involving a 'coronet'. One such scandal involved another of our forebears, the Marquess of Dufferin and Ava, a former Viceroy of India. He had been persuaded by Whitaker Wright, subsequently unmasked as a fraudster, to become Chairman of the London and Globe Finance Corporation and when it crashed in 1900, the result was disastrous for the many shareholders, including the Marquess.

If this set-back had knocked the wind out of Beech's sails, he showed no sign of it as he bounded down the gang plank in New York just before Christmas 1904. As usual, his arrival was eagerly reported by the press and ' The American' tells us that his brother Edmund, Edward Lowndes Rhett and his cousin Edmund Kirby, were there to meet him. During some high-spirited banter, Beech pulled from his jacket the photograph of a beautiful young lady. 'The future Lady Fairfax?' they enquired. 'Maybe so, fellows,' he replied. A tantalising snippet, but who she was we will never know, as we never hear of her again and it would be many years before Beech finally took our grandmother up the aisle.

Although the two years he had spent in London were not deemed a success as far as business went, they certainly marked a major turning point in Beech's life. If he was seen as something of a curiosity in New York, in London he was treated quite differently. It has always been the case that family and breeding are taken more seriously in England than in America, where money trumps all. So what a surprise and delight it must have been to Beech, a man of modest means, to suddenly find himself feted by the 'Great and the Good'. Invitations came thick and fast and none more sought after than from the King himself, to whom he was presented by Lord Kinnaird at a Court Levée in March 1903. Kinnaird, a fellow Scottish Peer and banker, was clearly quite a character. By then President of the Football Association, in his youth he had been a famous soccer player, taking part in a record breaking nine Cup Finals, famously standing on his head in front of the pavilion to celebrate a victory! The King was fascinated by Beech's unusual status as both an American and a Peer and the two spent several minutes in conversation, a great honour for a foreigner.

Another highlight of his time in London was the speech he gave to the 'Society of Yorkshiremen in London' in February 1904. Beech was keenly aware of the family's ancient links to 'God's Own County', as they proudly call it, so it was a great honour when asked to respond to the President's toast of 'Yorkshire, Our County'. His speech made much of the links and similarities between Yorkshire and Virginia, not least that both had produced so many leaders of their respective counties and had been the crucible of conflict in both the English and American Civil Wars.

With all this fuss being made over him, it is easy to see why Beech was beginning to feel so much at home in England. Here, as Lord Fairfax, he was treated with real respect and deference, allowing him to mix freely with the highest in the land. Back in New York, he was plain old Mr Fairfax, although it must be said he was by now rather more than just a curiosity and press interest in him continued unabated. Would he take the title, what were his loyalties? Although he continued to assert his loyalty to the American flag, the truth was, the 'Old Country' had cast its spell over him and slowly but surely he was being drawn inexorably towards it.

However, there was a fly in the ointment. During his time in England he had discovered that while he was generally accepted as a Lord, he would have to prove it legally to enjoy the privileges of a Peer of the Realm, such as a seat in Parliament. (Actually the title was in the Peerage of Scotland and under the terms of the 1707 Anglo-Scottish Union, it did not carry with it automatic membership of the House of Lords. After every general election, the Peers of Scotland elected 16 of their number to represent them in the new parliament.) What is more, he would also have to become a British subject, renouncing his American citizenship once and for all. Proving his claim was one thing, but giving up his American birth right was quite another – it would mean turning his back on his family, his friends and an American heritage that stretched back over one and a half centuries. This was no small matter, in fact it would be a life changing decision for Beech and his family. Would it really be worth giving up all that, just for the sake of a title?

This was the question Beech would wrestle with in the coming years. Knowing what we do of the man - that he was unassuming, level-headed and hard-working, it seems odd that he would even contemplate any move that was not based on sheer good business sense. But that would be to overlook his motives and ambitions. There is no doubt that his trips to England had opened his eyes to another world, and one with a different set of values. It would have been odd for him not to be entranced to some extent by the attention and respect he had received in England. More to the point, deep inside there burned his overwhelming ambition to re-establish the family to its former prominence and fortune. Perhaps he could best achieve this in England?

Writing now as a 21st Century Englishman, after two terrible world wars and a century of decline, it is easy to forget what Great Britain meant in the Edwardian Era. Then Britannia really did rule the waves. Her empire straddled the globe and this little island in the North Atlantic was the most powerful country in the world, both economically and militarily. The City of London was at the very hub and the tentacles of its institutions reached into every corner of the globe. Taking an opportunity to enter the pinnacle of society in the most important place in the world, by becoming British, was not so very odd as it might now appear.

Meanwhile, back in New York he continued to work for the International Banking Corporation, but things had changed. Gone were those days of just getting-by. He was now reputed to be a man of means, although the claim by the New York Morning Journal that he had *'close on $1,000,000'* (maybe $26 million in today's money), should probably be taken with a pinch of salt (as with most things we read in the newspapers).

However when I say 'probably', perhaps I am not giving our remarkable grandfather due credit. Although it was quite impossible that he would have accumulated such a sum as a salaried employee of a bank, there were other ways he might have done so. Perhaps he had speculated successfully on the Stock Market, although that does seem unlikely given the careful man he was.

Another tantalising clue to his new-found prosperity crops up in the *Baltimore American* newspaper of 29th March 1904. Headlined, incorrectly, *'Fairfax Has Assumed Title,'* the article goes on to say, *'Albert Kirby Fairfax, the Marylander who went to England two years ago, has within the past four months been legally adopted by a wealthy Englishman as the heir to his estates, and was finally persuaded into wearing the titles which he is now able to support in a fitting manner.'* This is quite a claim and while it might possibly be true, no mention of this 'adoption' has ever been heard of since, so I feel we must again put this down to the journalist's flight of fancy.

Whatever was the case, there is no doubt that Beech was now doing well. As a hardworking bank manager on Wall

Street he was able to live comfortably. He was now a member of the Union Club, that bastion of New York's elite, while at the weekends he would play golf in New Jersey. He was obviously a popular member of the Union Club, whose members would have loved having a real lord in their midst.

We get a good flavour of life there from an amusing letter written to Beech by his fellow member J. Stewart Barney in 1904. At the time Beech was working in London and was behind with his dues to the Club, an honest mistake, but happily his friend stepped into the breach...to paraphrase: '*I suppose you are so busy dining with kings that the little formality of paying your dues to the Union Club has entirely slipped your mind...You will pardon the liberty I take in doing this, but it was at the suggestion of Old Thomas, who was very much exercised on the subject and informed me that his Lordship's dues were not paid (rolling it on his tongue with apparent pleasure) and that I, as a friend of his, should attend to it....I am raising the daughter with a great deal of care, and working hard, so that when you come over to claim Lady Fairfax, the marriage settlement will be satisfactory, I hope...You would have enjoyed it at the Club last night, in listening to the war talk. All of the fellows joined me in kindest regards to you and request that you use your good offices with your friend the King, to avoid the war with Russia, as we hardly feel the stock market is sufficiently strong to stand a presidential election and a foreign war the same year.*'

Incidentally, the amount in question was $100, no small sum in those days, and equivalent to the monthly rent of a very comfortable apartment in a good area of Manhattan, which just goes to show how well Beech was doing. Needless to say the dues were paid and Beech remained a member up until 1929.

Another colourful memento of good times at the Union Club in those days is a rather 'racy' menu card for a dinner there a few years later in 1911. Beautifully illustrated, this features a naked lady clinging to a pole topped by a polar bear, an allusion to the explorer Robert Peary's claim to have reached the North Pole two years before. Around the pole are caricatures of various members in fancy dress, including one dressed in ermine, robes and a coronet: no prizes for guessing who this might be! As for the naked lady, well that's anyone's guess, but they certainly seemed to be enjoying her company!

35. The Fork in the Road

Success had not come easily to Beech nor had it come overnight; all those years as a clerk at Brown Brothers were a hard school, but now in his mid-thirties he was at last reaping the benefits.

This was a good time to be young and ambitious. The world was changing fast and opportunities were all around. Those that came Beech's way, he seized with enthusiasm. The first was the opportunity to travel to the King's coronation in London, so fulfilling Andrew Carnegie's famous dictum that the rising man must attract attention to himself. Then came the opportunity to work as deputy manager for the International Banking Corporation in London, and now in 1906 the opportunity to become a partner of a Wall Street firm. This really was a defining moment for Beech: in six short years he had come from the back office to the boardroom – he had arrived!

The firm that gave him this opportunity was William P. Bonbright, a relatively new business founded in 1902. Its speciality was providing finance for the rapidly developing electrical industry, and business was booming.

As a matter of interest, general partners in Wall Street brokers were not personally required to put up any capital themselves as the firm itself had membership of the Exchange, which was just as well since becoming an individual member required very deep pockets. According to the distinguished economic historian John Steele Gordon, when his own grandfather became a 'member' in 1914, the cost was around $86,000, about $2.1 million today! So you either had to be very rich or very confident of your ability to pay off any future losses!

Like Beech's former employer, Bonbright had an office in London. Without wishing to detract from Beech's experience and professionalism, it was no secret that he saw his future in England, and he was a lord to boot, so who better to represent Bonbright there?

This was the opportunity he had been looking for. As a partner in a go-ahead Wall Street broker, he at last had a real prospect of re-establishing the family's fortune. Reclaiming the title would set the seal on his achievements and the name of Fairfax would once more stand tall in the world. He was determined to make that his legacy, even if it meant leaving his American family behind and becoming an Englishman.

Had he foreseen the dreadful calamity that would befall Britain and Europe just seven years later, then he might not have rushed into this decision with such haste; but of course hindsight is a wonderful thing!

So the die was cast and the years of prevarication were now over. Beech had at last made the momentous decision. He would become an Englishman and lay claim to the title that was rightly his: Lord Fairfax of Cameron, a peerage created by King Charles 1st for his forebear Thomas Fairfax in 1627, but ignored since the death of his great-great-grandfather Bryan in 1802.

In 1907 he set sail once more for England and began the long process of establishing his claim, which first of all meant taking British nationality. A prerequisite of this was to have lived in the United Kingdom for five years, and although he had spent several extended periods in New York, he had maintained a permanent London address at 22 Upper George Street, just north of Hyde Park, and this seems to have satisfied the authorities.

The momentous day finally arrived. On September 11th in 1907, Albert Kirby Fairfax, the scion of seven generations of American Fairfax's, formally renounced his birthright as a citizen of the United States of America. Placing his hand on the Holy Bible, he solemnly swore the oath of allegiance to Edward VII, King of Great Britain and Ireland and Emperor of India, and with that he became a British subject. The family had come full circle after an interval of nearly 150 years.

That was not all there was to it, as the process of naturalisation was long and complicated, and for an American, highly unusual. Here it is succinctly summed up in the English magazine Country Life, October 1907.

> *'The monthly publication in the (London) Gazette of the names of newly naturalised Britons generally shows a list of foreigners who have come from Germany and Eastern Russia. The list is never very long, not more than a hundred or so. Compared with the monthly naturalisations in the United States it is infinitesimal. It is very seldom that a citizen of the United States becomes a British subject and if he does it is perhaps because of business necessity; for there is no other reason why an American should convert himself into an Englishman. Socially it makes no difference and as for a vote, he can have all that (except for Parliament), including the doubtful privilege of serving on juries.*
>
> *It is however, another matter for a man who is the possessor of an ancient title like that of Lord Fairfax of Cameron to seek to obtain the full benefit of his naturalisation...Lord Fairfax, if he is put through the usual routine of nationalisation, will be harried up hill and down dale by officials of the Home Office, assisted by detectives of Scotland Yard. They hound the poor candidate for weeks. He has to swear all sorts of declarations as to his antecedents, his health, his morals, his financial position, his mode of life and what not; and when all these matters have been satisfactorily attended to, he has to produce five sponsors, British rate payers, who are to swear that they have known him intimately for years, that they know nothing to his detriment and they, themselves, come up to the standard set by the great Bayard, 'sans peur and sans reproche'...after which, in*

> *good time, The Right Honourable Herbert Gladstone, one of his Majesty's Principal Secretaries of State finds it a matter of grace in himself to admit the candidate to membership of the great British Empire.'*

Although the article in *Country Life* claims it was very unusual for an American to become an Englishman, there were other high-profile exceptions to this rule. In 1899, William Waldorf Astor had taken British nationality, declaring that *'America is not a fit place for a gentleman to live,'* and later in 1916, the writer Henry James would do the same, seeking *'Posterity not prosperity'*. Unlike James, however, Beech sought both and he would not be disappointed.

This was the first step towards re-claiming the title but it would be another year before he would finally seize his prize. Meanwhile business called, so late in November he returned to New York, although now of course an 'alien' and subject to all those checks foreigners were subjected to when arriving in America. How strange that must have been to someone who had been born and bred in America. It must certainly have brought home the full weight of his decision.

As ever, the Press was on Beech's tail the moment he set foot on dry land. Now the question was whether he had taken British nationality and strangely his answer was somewhat evasive: *'If it is, it is the first I've heard of it,'* he teased with a smile. Perhaps he was embarrassed to admit the truth, or maybe simply wished to avoid causing any offence. Of course his family were still American and he still owned Northampton, the family tobacco farm in Maryland, which he had inherited on his father's death in 1900. So to all extents and purposes he still belonged to America, and probably still thought of himself as an American, even if he was no longer a citizen.

Another subject close to the heart of the American press was his marital status. As an eligible bachelor, and a titled one to boot, the press seems to have decided that Beech was obviously in need of a wife. The question was, would he pick an English girl or an American? As one who had lived on both sides of the Atlantic, who better to explain the difference between the English and American variety, and his views on the subject appear in an amusing article of this time in the *New York American*, headlined '*There are No Lemons in the American Garden of Women.*' As Beech explains: '*The American woman is all nerves – nerves and nervous energy. Keen, alert, alive, she is the busiest and hardest working woman in the world. To me she is always working. Why, even her recreation is work to her. She is so strenuous she doesn't know how to have leisure. And the English woman? Oh, she never hurries; she takes time for everything. She sees no reason for struggling and rushing in order to accomplish the things she purposes to achieve. Yet after all, she accomplishes a great deal more.*' Of course, ever the diplomat, he refused to be drawn as to his preference: '*I must be strictly loyal to both sides.*' So we must draw our own conclusions, but as things turned out, he picked neither and married a Scottish lady, our grandmother Maud, although that would be several years in the future.

36. The Lost Pleiad of the British Galaxy – Restored!

It was not for more than a year that his claim finally came before the Committee for Privileges of the House of Lords, on November 17th 1908. The Committee was the body that decided claims to peerages and it would ascertain whether 'America's only Peer' could prove without doubt his right to the 'Title, Honour and Dignity' of Lord Fairfax of Cameron in the Peerage of Scotland. As we shall see, it was by no means an open and shut case.

The claim to a peerage was taken very seriously in those days, which is hardly surprising given Britain's pre-eminence as a world power. The House of Lords still wielded real influence and its members commanded immense prestige in turn. So when the Committee for Privileges sat down to consider the evidence for Beech's claim, it was no small matter and its members did their work with grave purpose. The Committee was presided over by Lord Loreburn (Lord Chancellor of Great Britain), the Earl of Onslow (Chairman of Committees), Lord Ashbourne (Lord Chancellor of Ireland), Lord Robertson and Lord Collins (both 'law lords' - equivalent to Supreme Court Justices). Representing Beech was Mr G. Woods Woolaston, a member of the College of Arms with the quaint title of Bluemantle Pursuivant of Arms in Ordinary, an office dating back to 1484!

As Bluemantle pointed out, the essential problem was that most of the family papers that might have been used to prove the claim had been lost or destroyed in the American Civil War. However, he went on, Beech was no upstart and despite their American birth, the doings of this family were regularly commented on by the British press. Every marriage, birth and death had been recorded as it occurred. In America too, the family had not lived in obscurity and one member of the family, Hannah, had married George Washington's cousin, Warner. Since his father's death in 1900, no one had ever disputed that Beech was indeed the rightful heir to the title. The peerage had many associations, interesting both in this country and in America, and the claimant thought it due to his family to substantiate his right to the title.

Beech's cousin Wilson Miles Cary had travelled over from America to testify on his behalf and he now described the cataclysmic events of the Civil War in Northern Virginia and the havoc it had caused. He recalled that when the war was over, he had looked in vain for the lost family papers on the battlefields near where the old family home, Vaucluse, had once stood. Neither were there any parish records to show when and where the various members of the family had been born; these too had 'gone with the wind'. In their absence, all he could produce was a certified copy of the inscription on the gravestone of Bryan, 8th Lord Fairfax, in Ivy Hill Cemetery, Alexandria. This was important, as Bryan had been the last member of the family to have proved his right to the title in 1800. Now Beech, his senior living descendant, was able to use that precedent to support his claim.

However he still had to prove his line of descent from Bryan and in the absence of any other records there was only one way left to do this. It had been a family tradition to list every birth in the front of the family Bible and luckily this volume had survived the disasters that had befallen the family over the years. With all due reverence, Beech carefully laid the Holy Book before their Lordships and here they found the evidence they needed.

What seems finally to have clinched it for Beech was the evidence provided by his cousin Caroline Snowden. A native born Marylander, Caroline had become a Catholic (which must have horrified her family) and joined the Sisters of Mercy, based at the Convent and Orphanage of the Faithful Virgin in Folkestone, Kent. The word of a devout nun could not of course be doubted and when asked by the Lord

Chancellor if she had ever heard of Beech's father having a son by a previous marriage, her reply to the negative seems to have swung the Committee in Beech's favour.

Summing up, the Attorney-General said that the only two points noted for criticism had been cleared up by her brief evidence. The Lord Chancellor then moved that the petitioner had made out his claim, '*To the title, honour and dignity of Lord Fairfax of Cameron in the Peerage of Scotland*' and the motion was carried 'Nemine contradicente' – unanimously approved! So, with that, the 'Lost Pleiad of the British Galaxy', to quote another of our forebears Lord Dufferin, was finally restored to its rightful place. How pleased Beech must have been!

Beech could now officially style himself 'The Honourable the Lord Fairfax of Cameron', as would his son Thomas, and now my brother Nicholas. However, as the title is a Scottish one, only those elected by their fellow Scottish peers could actually sit in the House of Lords and Beech would have to wait until 1917 for that privilege.

One wonders what people in America, especially his family, made of this curious turn of events? Under the barnstorming President Teddy Roosevelt, America had become an increasingly self-confident and prosperous nation. For a citizen to turn his back on the 'Land of the Free' was almost unheard of and would seem quite inexplicable. Why on earth would anyone want to give up such a magnificent birthright? So, Beech played his cards close to his chest when challenged on the matter. As for his family, one hopes they were proud of his achievements, although it is also easy to imagine their sadness at losing a son and brother to another country. The only hint of dissent in the family comes from a somewhat terse comment by Beech's brother Edmund in the New York Evening Journal: '*The fact that my brother has been made a lord makes no difference with our family.*' Perhaps Edmund was just a little envious of all the attention his brother was receiving? We cannot tell, but we do know that unlike his high achieving brother, Edmund's career did not flourish and although he eventually married, his life was rather a sad one. On a more positive note, the article goes on to say that Beech's many friends on Wall Street thought his title would be a great help to his business activities in London, although they still thought of him as a good American and his sympathies were with their country.

As to the other members of his family, Beech's mother, Mary Kirby Fairfax, passed away in 1912 and his sister Frances was widowed in 1913 when her husband Edward Lowndes Rhett also died. Happily, Frances remarried Clarence Roberts in 1917 and they would run the farm at Northampton on Beech's behalf.

Of Beech's other sisters, Josephine was married to Tunstall Smith and lived in Baltimore with her two daughters, Josephine and Louise. Louise, a nurse in World War I, died tragically young at only 23 but Josephine married Lee Barroll in 1918 and had two daughters and a son. His two other sisters never married. Mary Cecilia became a teacher in New York, while Caroline, the eldest, passed her days in Baltimore as something of a celebrity, holding court when anyone came to pay their respects. It is said that even Eleanor Roosevelt would call on her to seek advice. While her surroundings were not grand, she always maintained the highest standards and would insist that tea was served from the ancient Fairfax family silver service!

This stage in my grandfather's life ended with a sad and dramatic episode. Not long after his successful claim to the peerage, Northampton, the wonderful old family home in Prince George's County, Maryland, burnt to the ground. Many irreplaceable family treasures, such as paintings and documents, were lost. No one was living there at the time and foul play was never suspected. A new house was built on the site, although nothing to compare with that which had stood there before, and this was the house our father would eventually inherit. What a tragic loss it was, and coming so soon after Beech's departure to England, it seems almost as if the old homestead knew its time had come, its purpose served.

Epilogue

In some ways this is where the story could end. The family, or at least the senior branch of the family that bears the title, would be British from now on and as this book is about the Fairfax family in America, we could easily end here. However, it is not as straight forward as all that and in many ways Beech would always be at heart an American. His family was still American, he still owned Northampton and he would continue to make regular visits to America, except when interrupted by the First World War. Indeed, records show he made the crossing in 1910, 1912, 1913 and 1914. It was lucky that he did not choose to travel on the Titanic in 1912 or I might not be here to tell the tale! He did actually go on the Lusitania but not on its fatal last voyage. In 1915 it was hit by a German torpedo off Old Kinsale Head in County Cork, Ireland with the loss of 1,195 men, women and children. This shocking outage awoke America to the German threat and helped bring the United States into the First World War.

When the War was over, his visits to America resumed. In fact, he even risked a trip in 1917, dodging the German U-Boats, but as his business commitments in London grew, these visits tailed off. Despite this and living the rest of his life as an Englishman, he would never lose his rich Southern drawl and was frequently referred to as the 'Yankee Peer' – an erroneous nickname given his family's devotion to the Rebel Cause in the Civil War!

More to the point, Beech was still only thirty-eight when he claimed the title, and over the course of the next thirty-one years until his death in 1939, there was a great deal this remarkable man would go on to achieve.

Beech had settled down to work for his new firm, William P. Bonbright, in London. This was a man defined by hard work and if evidence was ever needed to prove it, a photograph we have of him at this time shows a very serious figure at his desk, in winged collar with pen poised; his expression tells us all we need to know.

Away from his office, what do we know of his new life in London? Settling in London in 1908, he had arrived at the very apogee of that distant golden age, the High Summer of Edwardian England. To be an aristocrat, even one of American birth obliged to work for a living, was a very splendid thing indeed. Everyone wanted to meet the new arrival and grand invitations came thick and fast. Not least among these was the one in front of me now: from the Lord Chamberlain, summoning Beech 'on His Majesty the King's behalf', to an 'Afternoon Party at Windsor Castle on 20th June 1908, from 4.30 to 7 o'clock'. Of course this was Royal Ascot Week, the height of the English racing and social calendar, and everyone who was anyone was there. Doubtless many unmarried ladies, and their mothers, studied this curious American with interest but sadly we do not know of any liaisons that ensued.

Beech was also a great joiner of societies and as a member of the Pilgrims, the Anglo-American friendship society, he was feted with a dinner in New York before setting off for England in 1908. Once there, he quickly re-established the family's ancient links with the county of Yorkshire, becoming an enthusiastic member of the Society of Yorkshiremen in London. He also became a freemason, a long family tradition, and it seems entirely appropriate that he joined as a member of the Fairfax Lodge at Guiseley in Yorkshire. As he pointed out in a speech at the time of his admission in 1908, every American President from George Washington up to that date had been a freemason. Later in the 1920s, he even seriously considered moving to Yorkshire when the ancient Fairfax seat, Gilling Castle, came on the market. Set in beautiful country in North Yorkshire, Gilling had been the home of a Catholic branch of the family, the Viscounts

Fairfax of Emley, until they became extinct in the late 1700s. However, he decided it was too far from his busy life in London and it was acquired by the monks of nearby Ampleforth Abbey, who still run it today as a preparatory school.

As time went by and with no sign of any romantic entanglements to report, the press soon lost interest in him. In fact, we hear little of his life over the next few years, and that is how he must have preferred it. Of course, the elegant Edwardian world he had found so beguiling did not last for long. It all came crashing down in 1914 when the old European powers set about their self-destruction. One wonders if Beech had foreseen these terrible events and the huge changes it would bring to his adopted country, he would have rushed so eagerly to renounce his American citizenship? But he had made his bed and would have to lie in it.

America eventually rose to the occasion as financier of the war effort and huge quantities of material were shipped across the Atlantic. J.P. Morgan initially made all the running and Bonbright, as an American firm with close links to them, would play an important part in this vital work, both as a financier of international trade credit and bond broker. While this may have been good for the United States, the war was a disaster for everyone else. Not only did it cost millions of lives but billions of dollars too and by the end the American Government had lent almost $12 billion to the Allies. It is startling to note that although some of this debt was cancelled, as late as 1965 Britain was still using 1% of its tax receipts to repay its debt to America.

The First World War changed everything. An entire generation of Europe's young men lay dead on the desolate battlefields, grim witness to a failed diplomatic system. Despite the ghastly trauma of those four years, Britain was less affected than some of the other combatants; it would take the Second World War to really finish Britain and her Empire off. The British monarchy had survived, unlike most of the European monarchies that had gone to War in 1914, and the old order still appeared to hold sway. But the truth was Britain would never recover the dominant role it had enjoyed for so long in world affairs and the baton was now firmly in American hands.

For better or for worse, Beech was now part of the Establishment, sitting from 1917 as a Scottish Representative Peer in the House of Lords. Thanks to his new found prominence and undoubted abilities as a banker, shortly after the war's end he was appointed chairman of a new combine, 'The Amalgamated Cotton Mills Trust', a grouping of cotton companies in Lancashire. Chief among these firms was Horrockses Crewdson & Co., a company which had been established in the late 1700s and epitomised the rise and fall of the cotton mill industry in Britain. By the early 1920s the cotton business was in sharp decline, mainly due to stiff overseas competition. Despite efforts such as this to keep it going, by the end of the 1930s the industry had begun its inexorable decline.

Then in 1922, at the grand old age of fifty-two, Beech finally married. Why he left it so late is not known – perhaps it was not until then that he felt able to support a wife in suitably lordly style. Maybe he had just been too busy. Our grandmother, Maud, was the daughter of a powerful Scottish businessman, James McKelvie, who had extensive interests in the coal industry. Doubtless he rather liked the idea of his daughter marrying a Scottish Peer, albeit one of American birth, and in 1923 Maud produced an heir, Thomas, our father, followed in 1925 by our uncle, Peregrine.

Maud was a flame-haired beauty with a character to match and together they made a formidable couple, dividing their time between a town house in Stanhope Terrace, just north of London's Hyde Park, and a beautiful country house near the coast in Essex called Comarques, formerly the home of the writer Arnold Bennett. Here they entertained their friends and Beech's business contacts, not least among them the Governor of the Bank of England, Sir Montagu Norman and his wife Priscilla, granddaughter of the 7th Earl of Abingdon.

Despite their very different circumstances and as we have heard, Beech and Montagu Norman had become friends while working at Brown Brothers in New York in the 1890s. Now with the encouragement of his old friend and the support of his prosperous father-in-law, Beech was at last able to strike out on his own, and in 1925, a new discount house, Fairfax & Co., came into being.

Discount houses no longer exist, their role superseded by modern banking practices, but in their day they enjoyed a unique and privileged position in the City of London. Closely associated with the Bank of England, they acted as intermediaries between the Bank and the 'accepting houses', the senior merchant banks. They were able to borrow money on preferential terms and issue Bills of Exchange to facilitate trade, hence their name of 'Bill Brokers'. It was an arcane, cosy world where the senior partners would go about their business in the City wearing silk top hats and everyone knew each other. It was also a highly profitable one for those allowed to enter it!

This was a very long way from those early days of struggle in New York. Seizing every opportunity that came his way, our grandfather had worked his way up from the back office of Brown Brothers and could now count himself among the City of London's elite: quite an achievement for someone who had arrived in New York aged 18 after only three years of schooling and with only $25 in his pocket.

It goes without saying that Beech was a very driven man, but what really drove him on was the desire to restore the

Fairfax family's position in the world. Those humbling early experiences of his childhood in Maryland and then New York had given him a burning ambition to succeed and this he certainly did. He had reclaimed the family's ancient title and by now was more than financially secure, so at last he could devote his life to replacing all those treasures the family had lost in the American Civil War and then the disastrous fire at the family home, Northampton, Maryland in 1909.

Never a man to do things by halves, Beech now set about the task with his customary zeal. Over the next twenty years, right up until his death in 1939, a network of agents and dealers sought out everything and anything connected with the family and Beech bought whatever came his way. Family portraits, silver and fine furniture, but most of all he bought letters, documents and books, thousands upon thousands of them. The largest part of the library was a collection of over 5,000 'tracts' - propaganda pamphlets - from the English Civil War, equalled only in size by that held at the Bodleian Library in Oxford. More remarkable still were those documents from the Middle Ages, cataloguing the lives and times of the Fairfax family as far back as the 12th century. Beech commissioned a scholar, Henry Clifton, to translate these from the original Medieval French into English and they provide a fascinating glimpse into the lives of our distant ancestors. It seems they were serial litigators!

This fabulous library was really the culmination of his life's work, his crowning glory, and as I write these words the years roll away and I find myself transported back once more to where this story began, the library of our childhood home at Gay's House, Holyport, surrounded by the fruits of our grandfather's labours, his reward for all those long years of perseverance and determination. Beech never retired, it was not in his nature, but he enjoyed life and away from the office he was a devoted husband and father, played golf with a handicap of 18, was a keen shot and built his collections. These were not just of books and paintings: he also built up a fine wine cellar and among his papers was found a detailed account of every bottle he ever owned. He was still working in his seventieth year when he became ill and died shortly after the outbreak of the Second World War on 3rd October 1939.

He was buried in the village of Bilbrough, not far from York, just off the road to Tadcaster, on a plot of land acquired by the family in perpetuity. This charming village is at the heart of the old Fairfax family lands and close to two of the Fairfax estates, Nun Appleton and Newton Kyme. The most famous English member of the family, Sir Thomas Fairfax, the hero of the English

Civil War, is buried in the church next to the Manor, which in 1939 was still lived in by Guy Fairfax, a descendant of Admiral Sir Robert Fairfax who had purchased the estate from his distant cousin Thomas 6th Lord Fairfax. 'the Virginian Baron', in 1716. So here lies our remarkable grandfather, the Marylander returned at last to the land of his ancestors where he rests in peace for all eternity.

Beech lived long enough to see his two sons enter their teenage years but as the eldest, our father Tom was aged only 16, they were far too young to take over the family business. There was no successor within the business so it fell to our grandmother Maud to resolve matters; as the Battle of Britain raged above and the bombs rained down on London, she began negotiations with the Governor of the Bank of England, Beech's old friend Sir Montagu Norman, over the future of Fairfax & Co. In a lengthy exchange of letters held in the archives of the Bank of England, we see how the Governor urged our grandmother to merge the business with another discount house. Canny Scot that she was, she shrewdly resisted the idea, guessing that her interests and those of her sons would not be best served as 'sleeping' partners in a business they had no control over. So that was that, and at the very end of 1940, after months of fruitless discussions, the exasperated Governor had no choice but to agree and in Britain's darkest hour, Fairfax & Co ceased trading.

Our father Tom and his younger brother Perry were both sent to Eton College, in sharp contrast to their father who only attended school in Maryland for three years. Despite its reputation as a school for the cream of society it has always been a very tough school where new boys waited upon their seniors in a system known as 'fagging'; woe betide any 'fag' who disobeyed his 'fag-master's' orders - corporal punishment was commonplace and freely administered by teachers and senior boys alike. However tough it might have been, it instilled in the boys a strength of character that would stand them in good stead, particularly as Britain's fate was now seriously in doubt. As soon as they could, the boys joined up and so in 1941 we find our father a young officer in the Grenadier Guards, as part of the Guards Armoured Division. His brother Perry would follow him into the Army as a subaltern in the 12th Lancers, a famous cavalry regiment. He saw action in Northern Italy at the war's end and distinguished himself as the first British officer to cross the River Panaro, a tributary of the Po, leading a band of Italian partisans.

Our father never saw action, having been invalided out of active service after contracting a life threatening illness while training for the invasion of France. This was just as well, for his replacement was killed in action shortly after landing in Normandy. He had another lucky escape when stationed at Wellington Barracks, near Buckingham Palace in 1944. On 18th June a Flying Bomb scored a direct hit on the Guards Chapel during Sunday Service killing 121 of those inside. He should have been there too, but as luck would have it, that very morning he had been sent to another barracks, unbeknownst to our grandmother and uncle who spent a harrowing time searching through the rubble for his body. It is said that when the dust settled, the candles on the altar were still burning.

After the 1945 general election, Tom, now 13th Lord Fairfax of Cameron and still only 22 years old, was elected to serve as a Scottish Representative Peer in the House of Lords and embarked on a career in politics. As Parliamentary Private Secretary to the Lord President of the Council, Lord Woolton and then Lord Salisbury in the early 1950s, he had the distinction of serving in Churchill's last government. Later he became a Lord-in-Waiting to the Queen. In 1951, Tom married our mother, Sonia Gunston, a beautiful former model and accomplished pianist, at St Peter's Eaton Square, London. Sonia's mother was the eldest daughter of the 2nd Marquess of Dufferin and Ava, whose father the Ist Marquess we met earlier. It was he who had suggested Charlie Snowden Fairfax, our Californian pioneer, be given back his estates in England. How pleased he would have been that Charlie's great-nephew married his great-granddaughter! Soon the family started to grow with the eldest, Serena, being born in 1952. Then in 1956 Sonia produced an heir, Nicholas, followed by the author in 1958 and finally Rupert in 1961. Tragically our wonderful father would never see his children grow up, for he died all too soon at the age of just 40 in 1964. He packed a lot into his brief life and even found time to build a wooden motor boat, 'Gannet', in the garage at Gay's House.

Although we were born into what appeared to be a thoroughly English family, a link with America yet remained. Northampton, the old tobacco farm in Maryland, was still in the family. This had been managed by Beech's sister Frances since their father's death in 1900 and had passed to our father on Beech's death in 1939. For many years the farm was run on a day-to-day basis by an old retainer called Willie, who knew a thing or two about growing tobacco and over the years had made Northampton famous for some of the best in Maryland. When Frances died in 1950 the responsibility fell to Tom, although in those days before jet travel, trying to manage a farm from over 3,000 miles away was never going to be an easy task.

Another problem for Tom was the state of the British economy. The Second World War had reduced Britain to a state of near bankruptcy and since 1939 Exchange Controls (or Capital Controls as they are called today) had been imposed as a way of restricting currency movements in and out of the country. Most people never travelled abroad and even in the 1960s the travel allowance was only £50 a year per person! Sterling was under constant threat of devaluation and the British Government of Harold Macmillan looked at every way to bolster its reserves. Those with foreign assets were an obvious target for the Treasury and it soon became obvious to our father that Northampton would have to go. When Willie the farm manager also died, he bowed to the inevitable and so just short of 100 years since Tom's grandfather had purchased it, Northampton was put up for sale in 1959.

The sale of Northampton finally brought the curtain down on the story of the Fairfax family in America, a saga which began in 1690, several generations before the United States came into existence. It ended during my lifetime in 1960. Today Northampton is covered with housing and nothing remains of that lovely old family home, save for some old outbuildings. But the Fairfax family is not entirely forgotten and if you ever find yourself in southern Maryland, you might care to drop by the charming old church of St Barnabas, Upper Marlboro. Next to the church you will see an elegant brick bell tower, and if you stand under the arch you will find inscribed the names of those members of our family who once lived close by at Northampton and worshipped in the church all those years ago: Our great grandfather, John Contee Fairfax and his wife Mary Kirby Fairfax, our great aunts, Caroline Snowden Fairfax, Frances Fairfax Roberts and Mary Cecilia Fairfax, and finally our grandfather, Albert Kirby Fairfax, the last of our American family.

They are all long gone, but now they are no longer forgotten.

The End

Index

A

A Fairfax Friendship 74
Abingdon, Earl of 220
Acadia 51
Adami, Mademoiselle 143
Addisson, Joseph 45
Alamo 93
Albert, Prince 164
Alexander, Chales B. 196
Alexandria 37, 46, 77, 84–85, 87, 89, 91, 96, 100, 103, 108–109, 112, 115, 118, 131, 142, 144, 150, 166, 212
Amalgamated Cotton Mills Trust 219
American Civil War 166, 221
American Loyalists 69
American Museum in Britain 62
Amos, Dr 157
Ampleforth Abbey 218
Andrews, Emily Roseville 155, 157, 176
Andrews, General T.P. 155
Andrews, Richard Snowden 157–158, 173
Annapolis 76, 157, 172
Anne of Bohemia 23
Appalachian 52
Appalachians 21, 49, 92
Appleton House 25
Appomattox 156, 172
Argonauts of California, The 120
Arrigoni, Patricia 15, 117
Ash Grove 67, 95–96, 97, 112, 115, 143
Ashbourne, Lord 211
Ashby's Gap 41
Astor, William Waldorf 195, 209

B

Bader, Douglas 12
Baillie, Olive Lady 72
Baker, George Fisher 195
Baltimore 155, 157–158, 182, 214
Baltimore Sun 175
Baltimore, Leonard Calvert 2nd Lord 20
Bank of England 187, 220
Bar Harbor, Maine 168
Bar Harbour, Maine 149
Barbados 31, 75
Barroll, Lee 214
Bath 8, 60–62, 66
Battle of Antietam 150
Battle of Bentonville 167
Battle of Cartagena de Indias 35
Battle of Fredericksburg 144, 152, 167
Battle of Gettysburg 150
Battle of Manassas 163
Battle of Naseby 12
Battle of San Jacinto 93
Battle of Seven Pines 167
Battle of Shiloh 129
Battle of the Boyne 22
Battle of the Little Big Horn 174
Battle of the Plains of Abraham 50
Battle of Williamsburg 167
Battle of Winchester 158
Bedford, Duke of 49

Index

Beech" \t "See Fairfax, Albert 12th Lord 221
Beggar's Opera, The 9
Belhaven 46
Belvoir 38–40, 43, 53–55, 56–57, 59–60, 63–65, 73–75, 77–78, 95, 106–107, 143–144, 160, 169
Belvoir's 39, 41
Benham, Calhoun 126, 129–130
Benham, Joseph 126
Benham, Robert 126
Bennett, Arnold 220
Berkshire 8
Berlin, Irving 140
Beverley, Colonel William 34
Bilbrough 23, 25, 222
bill brokers 220
Bird's Nest Glen 127–128, 134, 139
Black Tom 12, 18, 23, 42
Black Tom" \t "See Fairfax, Thomas 3rd Lord 112
Bloxham, James 60
Blue Ridge Mountains 21, 34, 40–41
Bluemantle Pursuivant of Arms 211
Bodega Bay 136
Bodleian Library 221
Bolton Percy 23, 25
Bonbright, William P. 206, 218
Bonbright, Wlliam P. 216
Bonnie Prince Charlie 22
Boston 56, 81, 83, 100, 102
Boston Tea Party 81
Braddock 47
Braddock, General 49
Braddock, Major-General Edward 47

Breckinridge, John C. 130
Brent, Senator J. L. 130
Bright's disease 9
British Army 22, 48, 65, 71, 154
Broderick, Senator David C. 129
Brown Brothers 182, 186–187, 206, 220
Brunswick, Prince Ferdinand of 51
Buckingham, Duke of 24
Bull Run" \t "See Battle of Manassas 147
Burnett, Frances Hodgson 191
Byron 12

C

Cable, Benjamin 196
Cadogan Riding School 9
Cage, William 29
Cajun 52
California 17–18, 94, 111, 117, 118–119, 120, 122, 124, 126–128, 129–131, 132, 134, 137, 138–139, 140, 142
California State Assembly 124
Calumet Club 197
Cambridge University 188
Cambridge, Duchess of 90
Camp Winder 149
Canada 49–51, 133, 164
Carlyle House 37, 47
Carlyle, John 37, 46, 76–77, 95
Carlyle, Sarah 46
Carlyle, Sybil (West) 47
Carnegie, Alexander 199
Carnegie, Andrew 50
Carrol, Professor 166
Carter family 32, 81, 198
Carter, Charles 34

Index

Carter, Robert 'King' 29–30, 34
Carter, Robert 'King' 68
Carter, Robert III 97
Cary family 198
Cary, Archibald 116, 141
Cary, Clarence 142, 147
Cary, Colonel Wilson 43
Cary, Falkland 142, 145
Cary, Hetty and Jennie 149
Cary, Wilson Jefferson 141
Cary, Wilson Miles 212
Catherine de Valois 23
Catherine of Aragon 23
Ceely's Plantation 43
Census of 1900 190
Chapman, Nathaniel 49
Charles I, King 9, 12, 18, 21, 42, 207
Charles II, King 12, 19–21, 72
Charles River 102
Charlotte, Queen 55
Chesapeake and Ohio Canal 173
Chesapeake Bay 21, 32
Child, Sir Francis 36
Chippendale 38
Christ Church, Winchester 67
Church of England 86
Church of St Mary Magdalene 62
Churchill, Lord Randolph 191
Churchill, Sir Winston 191
Churchill, Winston 156
Cincinnati, Ohio 119, 126
City of London 184, 203, 220
Civil War 12, 14, 17–18, 42, 67, 96, 108–110, 112, 116, 125, 131, 136, 141, 143, 150, 156, 174, 176, 180, 211–212
Clarke County 34
Clarke, John 75
Claverton Manor 62
Cleburne, Major Gen. Patrick 130
Cleveland, President Grover 139
Clifton, Henry 221
Clive of India 50
Colgate, Adele 195
College of the Atlantic 168
Collet, Sir Mark 188
Collins, Lord 211
Columbia College 112
Comarques House 220
Committee for Trade and Plantations 35
Committee of Privileges 211
Confederacy 109, 130, 150, 160, 162, 166, 168
Confederate Army 112, 115, 129–131, 172
Confederate Navy 116, 145, 151, 167
Congress of Alexandria 47
Connecticut 103, 125
Continental Congress 57, 81
convicts 32
Conway stream 35
Cornwallis, Lord 22, 66
Coronation 192–193
cotton 162, 219
Country Life 208
Craik, Dr James 91, 96, 142
Crescent Athletic Club 197
Crocker, Charles 169
Cromwell 12, 19–20, 110
Cuba 50, 52, 163
Culpeper 20, 23, 29, 68, 72
Culpeper County 157
Culpeper, Catherine 20, 29
Culpeper, Thomas, Lord 19
Custis, George Washington P.

231

115
Custis, Martha Dandridge 44

D

d'Hauteville, Frederick 196
Davies, George 116
Davis, Jefferson 116
Davis, President Jefferson 149, 168
Defoe, Daniel 27
Degges family 173
Delaware 97, 149
Denton 23, 25
Dinwiddie, Robert 49
Dixon, James 136, 139
Dogue Run 38
Douglas, Stephen A. 130
Dufferin & Ava, Marquess of 133
Dufferin and Ava 10, 200
Dufferin and Ava, Marquess of 213
Dulles Access Road 95
Dumas, Alexander 168

E

Edward VII, King 192–193, 208
English Civil War 221
Episcopal Church 73, 87, 96, 138
Erskine, Lord Chancellor 89–90
Eton College 8, 11, 187

F

Fairfax & Co. 220
Fairfax Boulevard 18
Fairfax City, Virginia 18
Fairfax County 18, 37, 67, 76, 81, 86, 112, 114, 167
Fairfax Historical Society 122
Fairfax House, Alexandria 144
Fairfax House, York 25
Fairfax Lodge, The 217
Fairfax Militia 76
Fairfax of Emley, Viscount 218
Fairfax Resolves 81
Fairfax Volunteers 115
Fairfax vs. Virginia 32
Fairfax, Ada (Benham) 119, 126–127, 134, 136–137, 139
   death 139
   grave 170
Fairfax, Admiral Donald McNeil 108, 160–161, 163, 165
Fairfax, Admiral Robert 25, 30
Fairfax, Admiral Sir Robert 222
Fairfax, Albert 109, 111, 118, 154, 167, 190
   death 119
Fairfax, Albert 12th Lord 14, 99, 103, 111, 145, 174, 178, 203, 207
Fairfax, Albert 12th Lord ('Beech') 170, 172, 174, 176, 178, 180–181, 182, 184, 186–204, 206–209, 210–221
Fairfax, Ann 37, 39
Fairfax, Ann Caroline (Herbert) 112, 115
Fairfax, Anne 32
Fairfax, Archibald Blair 167
Fairfax, Aurelia (Irwin) 109, 116, 120, 144
Fairfax, Billy 77
Fairfax, Brian 24–25
Fairfax, Bryan 8th Lord 38, 46, 63, 73–75, 84, 89–91, 160, 207, 212
   birth & education 75
   children 77

Index

death 92
marriage 76
ordination 73, 87
succession 87
visits England 88
Fairfax, Bryan, 8th Lord
gravestone 212
Fairfax, California 15, 117, 118
Fairfax, Caroline 171–172, 173, 175–176, 190, 214
Fairfax, Caroline (Snowden) later Sanders 179
death 190
Fairfax, Caroline Eliza (Snowden) later Sanders 109, 111, 118, 137, 154–155, 171–172
Fairfax, Charles 174
Fairfax, Charles 10th Lord 15, 111, 117, 118–119, 120, 122, 132, 137, 139, 170–171, 174, 207
Fairfax, Charlie 10th Lord 119, 120–121, 123, 124, 126–128, 130, 132 134, 136–137, 141, 142, 170–171
birth 118
death 138
Fairfax, Col. William 65
Fairfax, Colonel William 29, 32, 34, 39, 46, 48, 50, 53–54, 63, 73, 76, 95, 99, 144, 154
Fairfax, Deborah 39
Fairfax, Deborah (Clarke) 38, 50
Fairfax, Dr Orlando 109, 115, 144–145, 152, 167
Fairfax, Dr William Henry 167
Fairfax, Edmund 171, 174, 190, 200, 213
Fairfax, Edward 12
Fairfax, Elizabeth (Blair Cary) 106

Fairfax, Elizabeth (Cary) 76–77, 95
death 86
Fairfax, Ethelbert 109, 167
Fairfax, Eugene 167
Fairfax, Eugenia (Mason, Hyde) 109, 116, 120, 143, 147
Fairfax, Ferdinando 58, 64–65, 77, 91, 95, 105–109, 160
Fairfax, Ferdinando 2nd Lord 18
Fairfax, Frances 171, 175, 190, 197, 214
wedding 197
Fairfax, George William 37, 39–40, 43–44, 48, 49, 52–55, 57–58, 60–64, 66, 69, 74–77, 106, 145, 160
Fairfax, Guy 222
Fairfax, Henry 30, 53, 73, 96, 109, 112–113, 114–115, 167
Fairfax, Henry 4th Lord 24
Fairfax, Herbert 167
Fairfax, Hon. Frances 36
Fairfax, Hon. Mary 23, 36
Fairfax, Isabella (McNeil) 108
Fairfax, Isabella (McNeill) 160
Fairfax, Jane 90
Fairfax, John 11th Lord 111, 118, 120, 137, 141, 142, 154–155, 157–158, 170–172, 173–174, 176, 179–180, 188
death 190, 192
Fairfax, Josephine 171–172, 173, 190
Fairfax, Lavinia 109
Fairfax, Lieut. Reginald 109, 116, 145, 151, 167
Fairfax, Louisa (Washington) 95, 100
Fairfax, Margaret (Herbert) 37,

Index

95, 100, 109, 112, 120, 142, 145
Fairfax, Martha (Collins) 36
Fairfax, Mary 171, 174
Fairfax, Mary (Aylett) 95, 99
Fairfax, Mary (Kirby) 141, 171, 174, 190, 214
Fairfax, Mary (Randolph Cary) 115
Fairfax, Mary Cecilia 214, 225
Fairfax, Mary or Cecilia 190
Fairfax, Maud (McKelvie) 210, 219
Fairfax, Minnesota 18
Fairfax, Missouri 18
Fairfax, Monimia (Cary) 109, 116, 120, 141, 142, 145, 147, 149, 167
Fairfax, Monimia (Davies) 116
Fairfax, Nicholas 14th Lord 213
Fairfax, Ohio 18
Fairfax, Oklahoma 18
Fairfax, Peregrine 219
Fairfax, Randolph 115, 167
Fairfax, Raymond 109, 167
Fairfax, Reginald 145
Fairfax, Robert 7th Lord 53, 69, 73
   death 87
Fairfax, Robert 10th Lord 36
Fairfax, Rupert 170
Fairfax, Sally 77–80, 84, 86, 95
Fairfax, Sally (Cary) 43–45, 49, 55, 58, 60, 62–64, 74, 76
Fairfax, Sarah 46
Fairfax, Sarah (Walker) 37
Fairfax, Sir Guy 12
Fairfax, Sir Nicholas 12
Fairfax, Sir William 12
Fairfax, Sonia (Gunston) 9, 133
Fairfax, South Carolina 18
Fairfax, South Dakota 18
Fairfax, Thomas 39
Fairfax, Thomas 1st Lord 23, 207
Fairfax, Thomas 3rd Lord 12, 18, 23, 42, 50, 108, 143, 180, 222
Fairfax, Thomas 4th Lord
   grave 67
   legacy 68
Fairfax, Thomas 5th Lord 21, 23, 25, 73
Fairfax, Thomas 6th Lord 21–22, 23, 25, 28–29, 32, 48, 51
   death 66
Fairfax, Thomas 9th Lord 77–78, 84, 86, 95–96, 98, 100–101, 103, 104, 106, 109, 119, 124, 141, 146, 160
   death 112
Fairfax, Thomas 13th Lord 9, 133, 213, 219
Fairfax, Victoria (Neave) 117
Fairfax, Virginia 15
Fairfax, West Virginia 18
Fairfax, William 30–32, 37
Fairfax, William Henry 38–39, 50
Fairfax, Wilson Cary 167
Fairfax's Company 113
Fantastic City, Memoirs of the Social and Romantic Life of Old San Francisco 125
Farewell to the Army of Northern Virginia 156
Farrand, Beatrix 168
Fauquier County 34, 144, 168
Field, Stephen J. 131, 139
Filmer, Edward 29

Index

First Maryland Artillery 157
First President" \t "See Washington, George 106
First World War 14, 151, 168
Flatiron Building 186
Florida 52, 93
Football Association 201
Fort Belvoir 39
Fort Cumberland 44, 75
Fort Duquesne 47
Fort Ross 136, 139
Fort Washington, Maryland 113
Fort Worth 148
Four Hundred, The 197
Frederick County 100
freemason 124, 217
freemasonry 138
French & Indian War of 1755 75
Frick, H.C. 199

G

Galt's of Washington 148
Gay, John 9
Gay's House 9, 13, 221
George I, King 27
George III 55
Gibraltar 25, 30, 71
Gilling Castle 217
Glenmore, The (ship) 120–121
Gold Rush 17, 94, 111, 119, 121
Golden Spike 178
Gone with the Wind 147
Gooch, Sir William 33
Gooch, William 31, 33
Gordon, John Steele 206
Gould, Edwin 199
Governor of the Tower of London 154
Grant, Ulysses S. 137

Grass Valley 122
Great Falls 76
Green Hill 95, 173
Greenhill Farm 77
Greenway Court 41–42, 48, 49, 51–53, 66, 70–71, 88
Grenadier Guards 9
Grove House School 182
Guadeloupe 51–52
Gunston Hall 39, 116
Gwin, Senator William 130

H

Hammond, Senator James Henry 162
Hanbury, John 49
Harper's Ferry 105, 146
Harrison, Archibald 196
Harrison, Burton 149
Harrison, Colonel Burton 116, 168
Harrison, Constance Burton 78, 84, 86, 116, 133, 141, 142–143, 145, 148, 149–150, 151, 158, 166, 168, 187, 195
Harrison, Fairfax 144, 168
Harrison, Francis 195
Harrison, Francis Burton 169
Harrison, Mary (Crocker) 169, 195
Havana 163
Hawling River 110
Henry VIII 23
Herbert, Margaret 46
Herbert, William 46
Hertford, Marquess of 132
Hicks, William 46
Historical Society of Pennsylvania 67
HMS Trent 163

Index

Holyport 8
Horrockses Crewdson & Co. 219
House of Lords 9, 74, 111, 180, 184, 188, 202, 211, 213
Houston, Sam 93
Howard County 110
Hyde, Charles 116
Hyde, Meta 143, 147

I

Ibbetson, Henry 25
International Banking Corporation 203, 206
Isle of Wight 11, 154
Ivy Hill Cemetery 91

J

Jackson, General Stonewall 157
James II 22
James River 43
James, Henry 209
Jefferson, Thomas 141
Joan of Navarre 23
Johnston, General Sidney Albert 129
Journal of My Journey over the Mountains 40

K

Kalbian, Maral 41
Kensington Palace 90
Kinnaird, Lord 201
Kip, Bishop William 132
Kirby, Edmund 200
Kirby, Minna 190
Knickerbocker Club 197

L

L'Enfant, Pierre 173

Lafayette, Marquis de 86
Lancaster County 29
Laurel, Maryland 111, 154
Lee 32
Lee, Colonel George 77
Lee, General Robert E. 37, 144, 150, 152, 156, 172
Lee, George 37
Lee, Harvey 128
Lee, Henry 107
Lee, Robert E. 144
Lee, Robert E. Lee 37
Lee, Thomas 49
Leeds Castle 20, 22, 23, 25, 28, 30, 36, 41, 48, 53, 55, 65, 66, 68–69, 71–72, 87, 88, 132
Leesburg Pike 95
Lefebvre, Hubert Pierre 146
Lewinsville 112
Lexington 81
Liberia 97
Lincoln, President Abraham 131, 149, 165
Little Hunting Creek Tract' 32
London and Globe Finance Corporation 200
Long Island 104, 196
Loreburn, Lord 211
Louisiana 49, 52, 93
Louisville, Kentucky 126
loyalists 86
Lusitania 216

M

Madras 37, 39, 51
Magna Carta 19
Maidenhead 8, 10, 117
Maidstone 23
Manassas Junction 147

Index

Manifest Destiny 92
Manila 169
Manor of Leeds 34, 41, 70
manumission 97, 107
March to the Sea 151
Marin County 15, 117, 126–127, 135–137
Marin Town and Country Club 140
Marlborough, Duke of 191
Marquis de Montcalm, Marquis de 50
Marshall Plan 156
Marshall, Colonel Charles 156
Marshall, Emily Rosalie Snowden 156, 176
Marshall, General George C. 156
Marshall, Sarah (Snowden) 156
Marston Moor 108
Martin family 36, 71
Martin, Anna Susanna 48, 71
Martin, Denny 69, 71
Martin, Denny (the elder) 48
Martin, Denny the younger 48
Martin, Edward 48
Martin, Frances 48, 71
Martin, Frances (Fairfax) 48
Martin, John 48
Martin, Philip 48, 71
Martin, Reverend Denny 88
Martin, Sibylla 48
Martin, Sybilla 71
Martin, Thomas 52, 57
Martin, Thomas Bryan 48, 71
Martin's Bank 188
Martinique 52
Martinsburg 71
Mary II, Queen 22
Maryland 14, 17, 20, 97, 109–111, 113, 116, 120, 130, 138, 141, 150, 154–155, 170, 172, 173–174, 176, 181, 182–186, 191, 197–198, 209, 214, 221
Marysville 123
Mason, Edgar 116
Mason, George 81
Mason, James Murray 163
Massacre of Glencoe 22
Massey 56
Massey, Revd Lee 55
McClellan, General 147
McKelvie, James 219
McNeill, Major General William Gibbs 160
Mercer, John 49
Mexican-American War 94, 109, 112, 155
Middleton, Mrs 89–90
Mills, General Giles 154–155, 176
Milner, William 25
Minden 51
Missionary Ridge 130
Monck, General 12
Monongahela River 49
Montgomery Castle 12
Monticello 141
Montpelier 111, 154
Morgan, J.P. 195
Morris, Gouverneur 196
Morton, Andrew 63
Mount Eagle 87, 88, 90, 108, 160
Mount Vernon 32, 37, 39, 43, 54, 60, 62–63, 78, 90

N

Napoleon 75, 93, 151, 157
Nassau 37

Index

Native Americans 22, 40, 47, 49, 51–52, 92, 135
nephritis 9
Neville, Amelia Ransome 125
New Jersey 104, 204
New Orleans 113, 150
New York 84–85, 92, 101, 104, 108, 130, 137, 149, 160, 168, 182–184, 186–188, 190, 193, 195, 197, 199–201, 203–204, 207, 209, 210, 213–214, 217, 220–221
New York Historical Society 166
New York Morning Journal 203
Newcastle, Duke of 33
Newhaven 103
Newport, Rhode Island 101
Newton Kyme 222
Newton, General John 148
Nicholas, Robert Carter 58
Nomini Hall 29
Norfolk, Virginia 100–101
Norman, Priscilla Lady 220
Norman, Sir Montagu 187–188, 220
Northampton plantation 171–172, 173–177, 178–181, 190, 197, 209, 214, 216, 221
Northern Neck 20–21, 25, 29–31, 33, 36, 38–39, 51–52, 66, 68–73, 97, 131
Northern Regulars 76
Norton, John 57
Norwich, Connecticut 103
Nova Scotia 51
Nun Appleton 23, 25, 222

O

Oaklands 111
Occoquan 55
Ohio Company 49
Ohio River 47
Ohio Valley 47
Onslow, Earl of 211
Oregon 94
Oriel College 23
Oriziba, The (ship) 130
Oxford 14, 23, 25

P

Palmerston, Viscount 164
Panama 121, 130
Panic of 1873 178
Pastori, Adele 140
Pastori, Charles 140
Patuxent Iron Work Company 110
Peary, Robert 204
peerage 53, 111, 188, 192, 207, 211–212, 214
Pell, Herbert C. 195
Pennsylvania 20, 67, 84, 97, 104, 120, 141, 150, 155
Personal Reminiscences of Early California 139
Peyton, Valentine 142
Philippines, The 169
Piedmont 106
Piercy, Charles 134
Pilgrims, The 217
Plan for Liberating the Negroes within the United States 107
Pohick Church 55
Pohick Creek 38
Polk, President James A. 93, 113
Pope, General John 157
Potomac 20–21, 31, 35–37, 38, 41, 46, 53, 61, 63, 65, 106–107, 131, 147, 169
Powers, Betsy 71

Index

Prentice, George 126
Prentice, Henrietta (Benham) 126
Prince George's County 109
Prince George's County 17, 155, 172, 176–177, 179, 197, 214
Privy Council 30–31, 33–34
Proprietary 20–21, 29–31, 33–37, 38, 41, 51–53, 66, 68–70, 72–73, 97, 131
Providence, Rhode Island 101–102
puerperal sepsis 155
Pulitzer Building 186
Putnam, General Israel 104

Q

Quakers 111
Quebec 38–39, 50–51, 76
Queen Eleanor 23
Queen Isabella 23

R

Rapidan river 35
Rappahannock 20–21, 35
Recollections Grave and Gay 141
Redness 53
Reminiscences of Senator William M Stewart of Nevada 122
Revolutionary War 126
Rhett, Edward Lowndes 171, 197, 200, 214
Richmond, Virginia 87, 100, 131, 145, 149, 152, 157–158, 168
Riggs & Co 173
Riggs National Bank 173

Riggs, George W. 158, 173, 178
Roberts, Clarence 171, 214
Robertson, Lord 211
Rock Creek Cemetery 139, 170
Rock Creek Church 138–139
Rockridge Artillery 152
Roosevelt, Eleanor 214
Roosevelt, President Theodore 213
Rotch & Tilden 168
Royal Ascot 217

S

Sacramento, California 118, 124–125, 128, 136, 138
Sagar, William 122
Sais, Domingo 126
Salem 31, 38, 99, 102
Salomon, William 199
Saltillo, Mexico 113, 115
San Francisco 117, 121, 124–126, 139, 195
Sanders, Colonel William 119, 142, 179
Scottish representative peer 219
Scribner's Magazine 168, 187
Seabury, Bishop Samuel 87
Second World War 9, 11, 154, 156
Semple, John 107
Seven Years' War 50
Shannon Hill 105, 107
Shannondale 106–107
Shenandoah 22, 34, 40–41, 46, 51, 68, 88
Shenendoah 100
Sheraton 38
Sherman, General William T. 151
Showalter, Daniel 134, 135

Index

Siege of Petersburg 151
Sisters of Mercy 212
Slidell, John 163
Sloane, William 196
Smith, Josephine 190, 214
Smith, Louise 190, 214
Smith, Tunstall 190, 214
Snowden family 109, 111, 154, 176
Snowden Hall 110
Snowden, Colonel Thomas 156
Snowden, Eliza (Warfield) 155
Snowden, Emily Roseville 155
Snowden, Gustavus Warfield 120
Snowden, Major Thomas 111
Snowden, Richard 120, 155
Snowden, Richard Nicholas 120
Snowden, Sister Caroline 212
Society of Yorkshiremen in London 201, 217
South Sea Bubble 27
Southern Railroad Company 144
Southern Railway Company 168
Spencer, Nicholas 29
Sprigg family 172, 176
Sprigg, Osborn 172
Sprigg, Samuel 173
Sprigg, Thomas 172
Sprigg, Violetta 173
St Lawrence River 50
Stanford University 131
Stanford, Leland 131
States Rights 150, 160
Steeton 12, 25
Stephen, Colonel Adam 71
Suez Canal 156
Sumner, General Edwin 129
Susquehannah River 104
Swedenborg, Emmanuel 96, 107, 146

T

Taliaferro, Alfred 121, 126–127
Teaninich Castle 169
Terry, David S. 129
Texas 93
The South will Rise Again 167
Titanic 216
tobacco 32, 46, 81, 96, 120–121, 173, 176–177, 209
Toulston 30, 53, 143
Towlston 62, 76–78, 80, 84, 87, 95
Towlston Grange 76, 87
Transcontinental Railroad 138, 178
Treaty of Guadalupe Hildago 94
Treaty of Paris 51, 70
Trent Affair, The 163, 165
Trenton 104
Tuck, Judge Somerville Pinkney 156
Tuxedo Park 195
Tyson's Corner 67, 95

U

Uncle Robert 175, 198
Uncle Tom's Cabin 146
Union Club 204
Union League Club 197
United States Military College 112
Upper George Street 207
USS Cayuga 165
USS Mohawk 165
USS Nantucket 165
USS San Jacinto 163

V

Valley Forge 84

Index

Vanderbilt, A.G. 199
Vanderbilt, Consuelo 191
Vaucluse 96, 112, 118–119, 131, 141, 142, 145, 147–148, 154, 166–167, 212
Vere of Tilbury, Lord 19
Victoria, Queen 144, 164, 192
Virginia 15, 16, 18, 19–22, 23–26, 28–32, 34–37, 40, 42, 46–48, 49–50, 52–55, 57–62, 64–65, 66, 68, 70, 72, 75–76, 78, 80, 82, 84, 86, 88–90, 92, 96, 97, 99, 102–103, 104–106, 112, 114, 120–123, 124–126, 131, 132, 138, 141, 142–143, 145, 146, 154, 168, 170, 173, 180, 187, 201, 212
Virginia Assembly 17, 68
Virginia Company 120–121
Virginia Militia 47, 49–50, 112

W

Walker, Major Thomas 37
Wall Street 182, 191, 199, 204, 206–207, 214
Walpole, Sir Robert 27, 35
War of 1812 65, 107
War of Jenkin's Ear 35
Warfield family 110
Warner, John 34–35
Warren County 34
Washington - A Life 81
Washington Boys Choir 171
Washington DC 15, 20, 49, 118, 120, 137, 139, 143, 154, 157–158, 173
Washington, Augustine 32, 49
Washington, George 15, 17, 22, 37, 39–42, 43, 47, 49–50, 54, 56, 58, 61–63, 66, 68, 74– 75, 77, 80–81, 87, 89–91, 96, 101, 108, 111, 115, 142, 180, 190, 211, 217
    letter to Lord Fairfax 82
Washington, Hannah (Fairfax) 38, 95, 211
Washington, John 95
Washington, Lawrence 39, 49
Washington, Martha 56
Washington, Mary 40
Washington, Mary (Ball) 32
Washington, Warner 38, 95, 211
Welles, Gideon 165
West, Hugh 47
White House 96
White House DC 65
White House, Belvoir 64
White House, Virginia 106
Wilkes, Captain Charles 163–164, 165
William III, King 22
William Penn 20
William the Conqueror 23
Williamsburg 33, 37
Winchester 41, 49, 66, 158
Windsor Castle 217
Windsor, Duchess of 110
Wolfe, General 38, 50
Woodburn 155, 172
Wool, General John E. 114
Woolaston, G. Woods 211
World War I 214, 216, 218
World War II 219, 222
Wrentmore, Elizabeth 169
Wrentmore, Margaret 169
Wright, General Horatio 148
Wright, Whitaker 200
Writhlington Manor 60–61, 63
Wykeham family 71

Y

Yankee Peer, The 216
York 193
Yorkshire 12, 23, 25–27, 30, 53, 57, 59, 62, 68, 76, 106, 144, 171, 201
Yorktown 22, 66
Yuba County 122–123

www.ingramcontent.com/pod-product-compliance
Lightning Source LLC
Chambersburg PA
CBHW072049110526
44590CB00018B/3094